THE NEW IMMIGRANTS

India

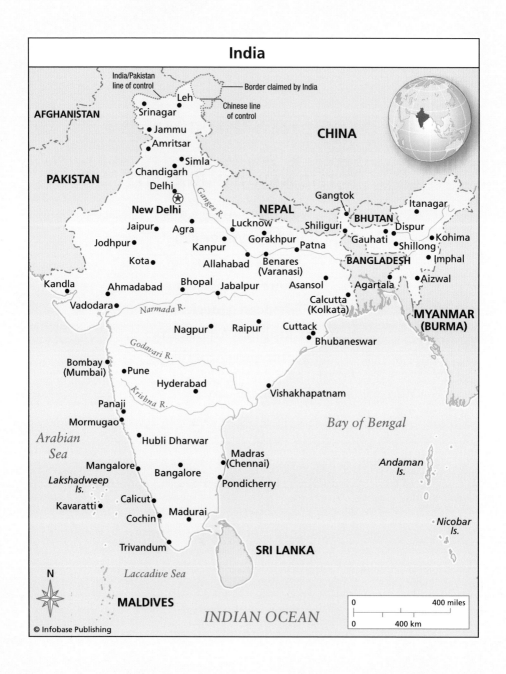

India/Pakistan line of control
Border claimed by India
Chinese line of control

AFGHANISTAN

Leh
Srinagar
Jammu
Amritsar
Simla
Chandigarh
Delhi

PAKISTAN

New Delhi

Jaipur
Jodhpur
Agra
Kanpur
Kota
Allahabad

Ganges R.

Lucknow
Gorakhpur
Patna

CHINA

NEPAL

Gangtok
Shiliguri

BHUTAN
Gauhati

Itanagar
Dispur
Kohima
Shillong
Imphal

BANGLADESH

Benares
(Varanasi)

Kandla
Ahmadabad
Vadodara

Bhopal
Jabalpur

Asansol

Agartala

Aizwal

Narmada R.

Calcutta
(Kolkata)

MYANMAR
(BURMA)

Nagpur
Raipur

Cuttack
Bhubaneswar

Godavari R.

Bombay
(Mumbai)
Pune
Hyderabad

Krishna R.

Vishakhapatnam

Bay of Bengal

Panaji
Mormugao

Andaman
Is.

Arabian
Sea

Hubli Dharwar

Lakshadweep
Is.
Kavaratti

Mangalore
Bangalore

Calicut
Cochin
Madurai

Madras
(Chennai)
Pondicherry

Nicobar
Is.

Trivandum

SRI LANKA

N

Laccadive Sea

MALDIVES

INDIAN OCEAN

0   400 miles
0   400 km

© Infobase Publishing

THE NEW IMMIGRANTS

INDIAN
AMERICANS

Padma Rangaswamy

Series Editor: Robert D. Johnston

Associate Professor of History,
University of Illinois at Chicago

CHELSEA HOUSE
PUBLISHERS
An imprint of Infobase Publishing

Frontis: India is the world's seventh-largest country and is home to 1.08 billion people. In 2005, there were more than 2 million Indian Americans living in the United States.

Indian Americans

Chelsea House
An imprint of Infobase Publishing
132 West 31st Street
New York NY 10001

Library of Congress Cataloging-in-Publication Data
Rangaswamy, Padma, 1945–
 Indian Americans / Padma Rangaswamy.
   p. cm. — (The new immigrants)
 Includes bibliographical references and index.
 ISBN 0-7910-8786-7 (hardcover)
1. East Indian Americans—History. 2. East Indian Americans—Social conditions.
3. Immigrants—United States—History. 4. Immigrants—United States—Social conditions. 5. United States—Emigration and immigration—History. 6. India—Emigration and immigration—History. I. Title. II. New immigrants (Chelsea House)
E184.E2R37 2006
304.8'73054—dc22   2006008384

Series design by Erika K. Arroyo
Cover design by Takeshi Takahashi

Printed in the United States of America

Bang FOF 10 9 8 7 6 5 4 3 2 1

This book is printed on acid-free paper.

All links and Web addresses were checked and verified to be correct at the time of publication. Because of the dynamic nature of the Web, some addresses and links may have changed since publication and may no longer be valid.

Contents

Introduction

Robert D. Johnston

At the time of the publication of this series, there are few more pressing political issues in the country than immigration. Hundreds of thousands of immigrants are filling the streets of major U.S. cities to protect immigrant rights. And conflict in Congress has reached a boiling point, with members of the Senate and House fighting over the proper policy toward immigrants who have lived in the United States for years but who entered the country illegally.

Generally, Republicans and Democrats are split down partisan lines in a conflict of this sort. However, in this dispute, some otherwise conservative Republicans are taking a more liberal position on the immigration issue—precisely because of their own immigrant connections. For example, Pete Domenici, the longest-serving senator in the history of the state of New Mexico, recently told his colleagues about one of the most chilling days of his life.

In 1943, during World War II, the Federal Bureau of Investigation (FBI) set out to monitor U.S. citizens who had ties with Italy, Germany, and Japan. At the time, Domenici was 10 or 11 years old and living in Albuquerque, with his parents—Alda, the president of the local PTA, and Cherubino, an Italian-born grocer who already had become a U.S. citizen. Alda, who had arrived in the United States with her parents when she was three, thought she had her papers in order, but she found out otherwise when federal agents swept in and whisked her away—leaving young Pete in tears.

It turned out that Alda was an illegal immigrant. She was, however, clearly not a security threat, and the government released her on bond. Alda then quickly prepared the necessary paperwork and became a citizen. More than six decades later, her son decided to tell his influential colleagues Alda's story, because, he says, he wanted them to remember that "the sons and daughters of this century's illegal immigrants could end up in the Senate one day, too."[1]

Given the increasing ease of global travel, immigration is becoming a significant political issue throughout the world. Yet the United States remains in many ways the most receptive country toward immigrants that history has ever seen. The Statue of Liberty is still one of our nation's most important symbols.

A complex look at history, however, reveals that, despite the many success stories, there are many more sobering accounts like that of Pete Domenici. The United States has offered unparalleled opportunities to immigrants from Greece to Cuba, Thailand to Poland. Yet immigrants have consistently also suffered from persistent—and sometimes murderous—discrimination.

This series is designed to inform students of both the achievements and the hardships faced by some of the immigrant groups that have arrived in the United States since Congress passed the Immigration and Naturalization Services Act in 1965. The United States was built on the ingenuity and hard work of its nation's immigrants, and these new immigrants—

primarily from Asia and Latin America—have, over the last several decades, added their unique attributes to American culture.

Immigrants from the following countries are featured in THE NEW IMMIGRANTS series: India, Jamaica, Korea, Mexico, the Philippines, Ukraine, and Vietnam. Each book focuses on the present-day life of these ethnic groups—and not just in the United States, but in Canada as well. The books explore their culture, their success in various occupations, the economic hardships they face, and their political struggles. Yet all the authors in the series recognize that we cannot understand any of these groups without also coming to terms with their history—a history that involves not just their time in the United States, but also the lasting legacy of their homelands.

Mexican immigrants, along with their relatives and allies, have been the driving force behind the recent public defense of immigrant rights. Michael Schroeder explains how distinctive the situation of Mexican immigrants is, particularly given the fluid border between the United States and its southern neighbor. Indeed, not only is the border difficult to defend, but some Mexicans (and scholars) see it as an artificial barrier—the result of nineteenth-century imperialist conquest.

Vietnam is perhaps the one country outside of Mexico with the most visible recent connection to the history of the United States. One of the most significant consequences of our tragic war there was a flood of immigrants, most of whom had backed the losing side. Liz Sonneborn demonstrates how the historic conflicts over Communism in the Vietnamese homeland continue to play a role in the United States, more than three decades after the end of the "American" war.

In turn, Filipinos have also been forced out of their native land, but for them economic distress has been the primary cause. Jon Sterngass points out how immigration from the Philippines—as is the case with many Asian countries—reaches back much further in American history than is generally known, with the search for jobs a constant factor.

Koreans who have come to this country also demonstrate just how connected recent immigrants are to their "homelands" while forging a permanent new life in the United States. As Anne Soon Choi reveals, the history of twentieth-century Korea—due to Japanese occupation, division of the country after World War II, and the troubling power of dictators for much of postwar history—has played a crucial role in shaping the culture of Korean Americans.

South Asians are, arguably, the greatest source of change in immigration to the United States since 1965. Padma Rangaswamy, an Indian-American scholar and activist, explores how the recent flow of Indians to this country has brought not only delicious food and colorful clothes, but also great technical expertise, as well as success in areas ranging from business to spelling bees.

Jamaican Americans are often best known for their music, as well as for other distinctive cultural traditions. Heather Horst and Andrew Garner show how these traditions can, in part, be traced to the complex and often bitter political rivalries within Jamaica—conflicts that continue to shape the lives of Jamaican immigrants.

Finally, the story of Ukrainian Americans helps us understand that even "white" immigrants suffered considerable hardship, and even discrimination in this land of opportunity. Still, the story that John Radzilowski portrays is largely one of achievement, particularly with the building of successful ethnic communities.

I would like to conclude by mentioning how proud I am to be the editor of this very important series. When I grew up in small-town Oregon during the 1970s, it was difficult to see that immigrants played much of a role in my "white bread" life. Even worse than that ignorance, however, were the lessons I learned from my relatives. They were, unfortunately, quite suspicious of all those they defined as "outsiders." Throughout his life, my grandfather believed that the Japanese who immigrated to his rural valley in central Oregon were helping Japan during World War II by collecting scrap from gum wrappers to make weapons. My uncles, who were also fruit growers, were openly hostile toward the Mexican immigrants without whom they could not have harvested their apples and pears.

Fortunately, like so many other Americans, the great waves of immigration since 1965 have taught me to completely rethink my conception of America. I live in Chicago, a block from Devon Avenue, one of the primary magnets of Indian and Pakistani immigrations in this country (Padma Rangaswamy mentions Devon in her fine book in this series on Indian Americans). Conversely, when my family and I lived in Storm Lake, Iowa, in the early 1990s, immigrants from Laos, Mexico, and Somalia were also decisively reshaping the face of that small town. Throughout America, we live in a new country—one not without problems, but one that is incredibly exciting and vibrant. I hope that this series helps you appreciate even more one of the most special qualities of the American heritage.

Note

1. Rachel L. Swarns, "An Immigration Debate Framed by Family Ties," *New York Times,* April 4, 2006.

Robert D. Johnston
Chicago, Illinois
April 2006

1

Who Are Indian Americans?

Have you ever been to a *Bhangra* party and watched people dancing in gay abandon to the heady beats of Punjabi folk music? Have you ever visited a restaurant where you were introduced to mouthwatering, spicy *tandoori* chicken served sizzling on a platter? Have you ever taken a ride in a cab driven by a *Sikh* wearing a distinctive turban or been served by a man named Patel at a convenience store or a roadside motel? Is your family doctor from Delhi or Mumbai, and does he or she speak perfect English but in an unfamiliar accent? If you answered "yes" to any of these questions, you have already been introduced to Indian Americans and their culture in ways you might not immediately recognize. If you are an Indian American yourself, welcome to this exciting exploration of your historical roots.

At the dawn of the twenty-first century, Indian Americans have entered every aspect of American daily life and made their mark on the American landscape. Still, in the minds of

11

Dr. Manmohan Singh, pictured here shaking hands with President George W. Bush during a visit to the White House in July 2005, became India's first Sikh prime minister when he was sworn into the office in May 2004. Today, the United States is home to more than 2 million Indian Americans, including more than 100,000 Sikhs.

many Americans, the word *Indian* is more likely to evoke images of Native Americans than of far-off India. When India's Prime Minister Dr. Manmohan Singh visited President George W. Bush in the White House in July 2005, he remembered this connection. He invited Americans to visit India and "complete the voyage" of Christopher Columbus who, in the fifteenth century, set sail to reach India and ended up discovering the North American continent instead.[1] Indians from India first arrived in the United States much later, in the nineteenth century, and since then, they have been called by various names, including "Hindu," "East Indian," "Asian Indian," and "Indian American."

At the time of Dr. Singh's visit, the United States was home to more than 2 million Indian Americans, an active and vibrant community of immigrants and their American-born children. They had come from an India that was a far cry from the fabled land of elephants, tigers, and snake charmers, the "exotic, oriental India" embedded in the American mind from the days of Columbus. The India that was sending immigrants to the United States in the twenty-first century was a newly emerging India. It was a proud, independent nation of engineers and scientists, nuclear reactors and space programs, and bustling cities and mega-shopping malls. Indian immigrants were settling in major cities and towns all across the United States, contributing to its progress with their unique skills, talents, and hard work. They were helping to transform their adopted country with their languages and cultures, foods and festivals, and religions and rituals.

A DIVERSE AND GROWING POPULATION

Indian Americans' diversity makes it difficult to define or categorize them as a group. Most of the world's major religions are represented in this ethnic group. They may be Hindus, Muslims, Christians, Buddhists, Sikhs, Jains, Parsis, or Jews. They are of hybrid racial stock, which means they could be either very light skinned or dark skinned and have a variety of facial features. They have been called "Caucasian," "Asian," or "white" at varying times in American history. Indeed, Indian Americans come not only from India but also from a wide range of countries around the globe, including the United Kingdom, South Africa, and countries in East Africa, the Caribbean, and the Pacific Islands. They speak many different languages and follow different customs, yet they have a common cultural bond that enables others to recognize them as a distinct ethnic group.

Even though they have been in the United States for more than a hundred years, the number of Indian Americans has grown dramatically only since 1965, when the Immigration and Naturalization Services Act allowed people from India to immigrate in large numbers. The Indian-American population grew more than four times, from 387,223 in 1980 (when they were first counted as a separate group in the U.S. census) to 1,678,765 in the year 2000.

This growth resulted from several factors, the most important being new immigration and already-established Indian immigrants having American-born children. The first group of Indian immigrants who came after 1965 were mostly skilled professionals, such as doctors, nurses, engineers, scientists, and professors. They were followed by their relatives, who were not as skilled and who took up jobs in the retail and industrial sectors as shopkeepers or factory workers. New immigration in the 1990s brought more "hi-tech" workers from India. At this time, the world had entered an era of globalization, when goods and services moved across nations more freely than ever before. India became a favorite recruiting ground for global service providers looking for engineering, marketing, finance, and healthcare professionals to fill vacancies in the United States.

Another factor contributing to the growth of the Indian-American population was the increasing number of university students from India, many of whom stayed on to become immigrants. India sent nearly 80,000 students to American universities in 2003–2004, a far larger number than any other country.[2] These students contributed to the U.S. economy in many ways, but mostly by bringing in large sums of money to finance their education and contributing their talents and skills in the American workforce.

The Indian population of Canada is about half that of the United States, or nearly one million, but because the entire population of Canada is only about 30 million, Indians represent 3 percent of the whole—a much larger proportion than in the United States.[3] Indian Canadians share a very similar history to

Indian Americans; they both arrived in North America more than 100 years ago. Like Indian Americans, the numbers of Indian Canadians grew dramatically in the 1960s, with the liberalization of Canadian immigration laws and the entry of skilled immigrants and their family members. Indian Canadians, too, settled mostly in the large metropolitan areas. Today, the provinces of Ontario and British Columbia are home to more than 75 percent of the Indian-Canadian population.

The major languages spoken by Indian Canadians are Punjabi, Urdu, and Tamil. Despite a legacy of cruel and blatant discrimination, Indian Canadians have achieved considerable material success and have entered mainstream Canadian life in a wide range of activities, among them as prominent businesspeople, politicians, and artists.

A SUCCESS STORY AND MORE

How did Indian Americans, who accounted for less than 1 percent of the U.S. population in 2000, become such a distinctly recognizable ethnic group? Some staggering figures show why Indian Americans became noticed in the United States. For one, they are the wealthiest and best educated of all ethnic groups. In 2003, more than 300,000 worked in Silicon Valley, California, the home of the computer industry, and they enjoyed an average income of $200,000 a year with a combined wealth of $60 billion.[4]

Major companies such as Microsoft, IBM, Intel, and Xerox, all giants of the technological era, relied on Indian Americans, who formed their largest pool of hi-tech employees. The father of the Pentium chip processor (Vinod Dham), the cofounder of Hotmail (Sabeer Bhatia), and the cofounder of Sun Microsystems (Vinod Khosla) are among the biggest names in the computer industry, and they are all Indian American. More than 5,000 Indian Americans serve on the faculty of U.S. universities. More than 35,000 Indian American doctors comprise about 6 percent of all physicians in the country. Indian Americans control an estimated 65 percent of budget motels and 40 percent of all hotels nationwide.[5]

Indian Americans play a prominent role in other interesting fields, too, and sometimes at an early age. For instance, they hold the record for winning spelling bee competitions, having taken first place in five of eight years between 1998 and 2006. As one journalist reporting on the 2005 contest wrote, "For many contestants, the most uncommon words at the national spelling bee last week were not appoggiatura and onychophagy, but the names of the top four finishers: Anurag Kashyap, Aliya Deri, Samir Patel, and Rajiv Tarigopula. All were of Indian ancestry."[6] These words reveal not only an admiration for the achievements of Indian Americans, they

In 2005, Anurag Kashyap, pictured here receiving congratulations from his classmates at Meadowbrook Middle School in Poway, California, defeated 272 other contestants from around the nation to become the Scripps National Spelling Bee champion. Indian Americans have won the spelling bee five of the last eight years.

also show how far Indian Americans have to go before they (and their names) become commonly accepted in American society.

When Indian-American children do well academically, their accomplishments are attributed to the drive and discipline instilled in them by immigrant parents and their belief in the power and value of education. Such stories of Indian-American success have served a double purpose. On the one hand, they have contributed to the pride and self-esteem of a comparatively new immigrant community, but on the other hand, they have also helped to create a stereotype of Indian-Americans as consisting only of high achievers—of doctors, entrepreneurs, engineers, scientists, and academics. Even when it is acknowledged that there are many who do not fit this profile, it creates yet another stereotype—that of the small-time motel owners, taxi drivers, and newsstand operators, or the bumbling, sing-song–accented Appu of *The Simpsons* television show fame. Indian Americans have spread their wings far beyond these stereotypes, though. There are more and more Indian Americans who are entering uncharted territories and embracing the full spectrum of career choices that the United States has to offer.

There are also many Indian Americans who do not fit the picture of the successful immigrant. According to the 2000 U.S. census, 27,947, or nearly 7 percent of Indian families, were living below the poverty line. Many of them can barely speak any English and are working in low-wage jobs or trapped in unemployment. How did they come to the United States as immigrants? What is their role in American society? As we explore these and other questions in the following pages, we will learn what draws Indians to the United States, what struggles and opportunities they encounter, how they have shaped their lives and raised their families, and what sort of future they might look forward to in their adopted homeland.

• Study Questions •

1. Describe some of your own images of India and Indian Americans.

2. How are Indian Americans generally perceived in the United States?

3. What are other names by which Indian Americans are known? Which do you think is the most suitable? Why?

4. Why are Indian Americans considered a diverse group?

5. Identify some factors responsible for the growth of the Indian-American population.

6. Name some languages spoken by Indian Americans.

2

The Punjabi Pioneers

Even before the major immigration started in 1965, Indians were coming to the United States, often without being noticed. There is the little-known story of Chandra Lachman Singh, who came to the United States from Grenada in 1911 and traveled to Chicago, where he worked as a dishwasher in a restaurant. He was drafted into the U.S. Army in 1918 and served in World War I. Between 1929 and 1932, he and his wife, Nerissa, traveled to India to work with the Indian independence movement. He lived in Chicago's Hyde Park until his death in 1989.[7]

Stories of many such individuals remain buried in history. The Indians who trickled into the United States were so few in number that they probably thought of themselves as pioneers. Hardly any would have been aware that there were thousands of Indians who had come decades before them under very different circumstances.

The history of Indians in the United States goes nearly as far back as the migrations of other Asian groups, such as Chinese, Japanese, Koreans, and Filipinos. As early as the nineteenth century, there were some scattered adventurers and merchants from India who visited New York and San Francisco to sell their wares. The Immigration and Naturalization Service records show a total of 696 arrivals from India by 1900. Among them were a few university students who came on scholarships and some political refugees who sought to escape British rule in India.

THE PUNJABI MIGRATION

The first big wave of Indian-American immigration began after 1900, when farmers from the northwestern Indian state of Punjab, driven into heavy debt by their British rulers, sought to escape drought and famine and looked abroad for fortune. They first learned about Canada from Indian soldiers who had crossed the country when attending Queen Victoria's Silver Jubilee celebrations in England. Attracted by stories of the high wages they could make working in the lumber mills of North America (more than 10 times as much as they could make on their farms at home), about 5,000 Indians came to Canada between 1904 and 1908, and more than 7,000 arrived in California between 1900 and 1910. These men were sojourners, who hoped to return home to their families after making some money abroad, so they came without their families. They sailed on a journey across the Pacific that took more than a month. They had to stop in Hong Kong or Fiji or Australia, because in those days, there was no direct steamship service from India to the American West.[8]

In the beginning, Indians were welcomed by their employers, who appreciated their hard work and found it profitable to hire them at lower wages than white workers. Soon, however, Indians faced the anger of native Canadians who accused them of taking their jobs, rioted against them, and drove them out of Canada with the slogan that Canada was for "whites only." The Indians fled south to the United States, to the lumber mills of Bellingham

Between 1904 and 1908, more than 5,000 Sikhs from the Punjab region of northwestern India were lured to Canada in hopes of earning higher wages in the lumber industry. Pictured here are Sikh workers outside the Northern Pacific Lumber Company in Barnet, British Columbia, in 1905.

and Everett in the state of Washington. Here, too, they encountered organized, racist violence from working-class whites. The Asiatic Exclusion League (which had been formed primarily to drive out the Chinese and Japanese from the United States) now also targeted the Indians. They denounced them as unclean and immoral and goaded townspeople to attack them.

On September 5, 1907, in what is known as the Bellingham incident, about 500 white workers broke into the waterfront bunkhouses in which the Indian workers lived, dragged them from their beds, and looted their belongings. The terrified Indians fled town en masse, fearing for their lives. At first, they fled northward to Vancouver in Canada but were turned back, so they made their way southward, down the Pacific Coast. Between 1907 and 1908, the railroads on the West Coast employed about 2,000 Indians. These men worked their way south until they reached California and settled down in a land where the warm temperatures and agricultural landscape reminded them of their native Punjab. Here, they were joined by other immigrants, who came directly to the United States from India. Around this time, there was also another small group of about 1,000 or so Indians who settled in the eastern United States and consisted of students, skilled workers, merchants, and traders.

PREJUDICE AND PAIN

Most of the early Indian Americans in California were Sikhs, followers of a religion that was born in fifteenth-century India as a blend of Hinduism and Islam. These men grew their beards long and wore the distinctive turbans required by their religion. Because of this, they were often ridiculed as "ragheads." There were also some Muslims among the Punjabi immigrants, but all Indians, regardless of their religion, were called "Hindus" by Americans, who did not differentiate among them. The Indians observed the strict dietary laws of their religion—Sikhs would not eat beef and Muslims would not eat pork. They spoke no English, so they clustered together, relying on a "gang boss" who spoke English and acted as a go-between with their employers. Because there were no women among them, they lived isolated and lonely lives, cooking their own food in crowded camps outside of town. They came to be seen by the townspeople as a strange and alien race, incapable of learning American ways.

In 1911, the U.S. Immigration Survey of Indian migrants in California stated that, "The East Indians on the Pacific coast are universally regarded as the least desirable race of immigrants thus far admitted to the U.S."[9] Public prejudice against them kept growing, and more and more immigration restrictions were imposed on them. In 1917, Congress passed a law, the Barred Zone Act, which specifically outlawed immigration from India. Many Indians who had hoped to send for their wives and children were disappointed, like this farmer, whose story is told in Ronald Takaki's *Strangers from a Different Shore*:

> Moola Singh had left his wife in the Punjab in 1911 and had saved enough money to pay for her passage to America. But by the time he had sent the money to her the (1917) law had already been enacted. "She worry," Singh told an interviewer many years later. "She good, nice looking, healthy, but she love. You know love, person no eat, worry, then maybe die. Mother wrote one time letter, 'she sick, you gotta come home.' Then I write her letter from Arizona, to her I say, 'I'm coming, don't worry, I be there…'" But she passed away in 1921 before Singh could return. "If we had our women here," said a fellow countryman, "our whole life would be different."[10]

Canadians, too, enacted laws meant to cut off immigration from India. The Continuous Voyage Act of 1908 barred the entry of immigrants who had not come on a continuous voyage from their native land. A wealthy Sikh attempted to skirt this law by hiring a Japanese ship, the *Komagatamaru*, to bring 375 Sikhs directly from India to Vancouver, but the Canadian government refused to let them land and deported them on other charges. Immigration from India to Canada dropped from 2,623 (1907–1908) to 6 (1908–1909). The ban was modified in 1919 to allow entry of wives and children, but as in the United States, immigration from India did not significantly increase until the 1960s, when laws were liberalized.

Other immigrants from Asia—Chinese, Japanese, and Koreans—were already in California in large numbers well before the Indians. The Chinese came after the California Gold Rush began in 1848, and the Japanese and Koreans came after 1880 to work as contract laborers in the agricultural economy. Reacting to their growing prosperity, the U.S. government passed the Chinese Exclusion Act of 1882, prohibiting admission of unskilled Chinese workers. The Gentlemen's Agreement of 1907 banned immigration of Japanese and Korean laborers. Many of the discriminatory laws were originally aimed against these other Asians, then applied to Indians as well.

Indians in California lived under very difficult conditions; they were subject to unfair laws that barred them from owning property, marrying whites, and becoming citizens. Despite this, however, they managed to become prosperous, raise families, and live productive lives. How they overcame barriers is a little-known story of courage and ingenuity that has yet to find due recognition in the history books.

THE ALIEN LAND LAW

The 1913 California Alien Land Law, strengthened in later years, specifically forbade immigrants who were ineligible for citizenship from owning property. This hurt all Asians particularly, because, once the railroads were built, the railroad builders turned to farming, but they were not allowed to own the land they worked on. Still, they rose quickly from merely laboring on the farms to leasing the land. The California State Commission of Immigration and Housing took note of this trend: "The change from employed to employer or lessee is rapidly placing the Hindu in the position of 'little landlord.' The Hindu will not farm poor land. He wants the best and will pay for it. Consequently, the American owner who can get a big rental for his land desires the Hindu. He will pay."[11]

The Alien Land Law was tightened in 1920, and even leasing of property was banned for Asians. Indians worked around this law by entering into business partnerships with white farmers and becoming part owners of the business. In these paper transactions, Indians and whites appeared to be equal partners but it was the Indians who did most of the work, whites merely lent their names and legal legitimacy. Whites were only too happy to partner with Indians who had gained a reputation for being "excellent farmers, very industrious, willing to work under trying conditions."[12] As soon as it became possible, Indians transferred ownership of the land to their American-born children, and thus gained full control of their property. Indians were a major factor in developing the agricultural economy throughout California—the sugar beet farms of Chico, the rice fields of Sacramento, the vineyards of Fresno, and the orchards of the San Joaquin Valley. Many of them moved to Arizona and turned the arid desert land into profitable rice fields, using farming techniques they had learned in India. They became so prosperous that they were known as the "Hindu rice kings."

THE MARRIAGE LAWS

There were marriage laws, too, that worked against Indian immigrants. Antimiscegenation laws were enacted to prevent mixing of races; they barred Indian men from marrying white women. The Cable Act (enacted in 1922 and repealed in 1931) took away a white woman's citizenship if she married an alien ineligible for citizenship. Prevented from marrying white women, Indians took Mexican wives, and raised Punjabi-Mexican families. It was a small community, of little more than a hundred or so families, but they acquired a distinct bicultural identity, which was reflected in the names of their children, names such as Carmelita Sidhu and Cirilia Singh.[13]

Because Sikh men were prohibited from marrying American women, many married Mexican women instead. Pictured here are the Mexican wives of Sikh men in Yuba City, California, during the First Indian Independence Day: (*back row from left*) Josephine Romo Subhra, Della Spence Khan, Alejandra Beltran Singh, Inez Wiley Singh, Cruz Perez Singh Ardave, Isabel Sidhu, Cirila Singh Chand, Nand Kaur Singh, Velia Riveria Sidhu, and Dorothy Sexton Sahota; (*front row from left*) Socorro Singh, Margarita Singh, Mrs. Mildren Geno Bains, Rosario Virgen Singh Gill, Mariana Singh, Antonia Alvarez Singh, Genobebe Loya Singh, Mary Singh Gill Rai, Amelia Camacho Bidasha, and Nina Singh Shine.

Punjabi fathers were often strict disciplinarians who wanted their sons to follow in their footsteps, but through their mothers, the children learned Mexican ways and the Catholic religion. Sons were expected to work for their fathers, and in the words of one Punjabi-Mexican teenager, "From the time I was twelve, I worked in the fields; Dad sent me to help other Punjabis and I seldom got paid for that." Tensions often arose when the children became adults and wanted to exercise freedom to marry a person of their choice or pursue a career other than farming. One daughter said of her father's expectations, "Marriage to a rich Hindu farmer was the idea he had for me." Another said,

"Father tried to fix me up with someone; he had land and we had land and that meant it'd be a good marriage."[14] Most members of the second generation married to please themselves, though, and often outside the Punjabi-Mexican community. Small as it was, the Punjabi-Mexican community showed the resilience of the immigrants in the face of discriminatory laws and added yet another colorful piece to the American multicultural mosaic.

CITIZENSHIP RIGHTS DENIED

The third front on which the early Indian immigrants had to struggle was citizenship rights. A 1790 federal law reserved citizenship for "whites only." In early court rulings (1910 and 1913), Indians were declared eligible for citizenship because they were considered Caucasian just like Europeans, but in 1923, in a dramatic reversal, the Supreme Court ruled that Indians were not "free white persons" and therefore could not become citizens. Many Indians had already become naturalized by this time and the government tried to take away their citizenship. One such immigrant, Vaisho Das Bagai, whose citizenship was revoked and who was stripped of his property, committed suicide in despair.[15]

Others fought back, however. Sakharam Ganesh Pandit (1875–1959), an American citizen and a lawyer, successfully fought off the government's repeated efforts to strip him of his naturalization certificate. He argued that he had always been an upstanding citizen, and the cancellation of his citizenship would deprive him of his livelihood and his property, and it would endanger his marriage. (He was married to a white woman.) Following Pandit's legal victory in 1927, the government canceled all further denaturalization proceedings. Pandit's courageous stand helped the fight against the government's racist ideas, and enabled countless others to enjoy the fruits of citizenship.

Indians still felt unwelcome in the United States, however. Between 1920 and 1940, about 3,000 Indians returned to India. Not until 1946, with the passage of the Luce-Cellar Bill, did Indians

(continues on page 30)

DALIP SINGH SAUND (1899–1973):
THE FIRST INDIAN-AMERICAN CONGRESSMAN

A rarity in American history, the first Asian and the first native of India to become a U.S. Congressman, Dalip Singh Saund is all the more remarkable for having achieved this in an era of restrictive immigration laws and strong prejudice against Asians. This Democratic Representative served three terms, from 1957 to 1963, and as a member of the influential Foreign Relations Committee, he traveled to India as a goodwill ambassador for American democracy.

Born into a well-to-do Sikh family of landowners in Amritsar, Punjab, Saund earned a Bachelor of Arts degree from Punjab University but saw no future for himself in an India dominated by foreign rule. An admirer of Mahatma Gandhi, Abraham Lincoln, and Woodrow Wilson, he decided to come to the United States, the "land of idealists and doers," as he called it, for advanced study. He continued, "Here I was a free man in a free country. I could go where I wished and say what I pleased." Unlike his fellow Sikh immigrants, he was highly educated, attaining a Ph.D. from the University of California, but like them, he earned his living as a farmer, in the lettuce fields of Westmoreland. He also manufactured and sold chemical fertilizers. During the Great Depression, his business slumped badly, and he almost went bankrupt, but he chose to pay off his debts over the next several years. He applied for citizenship as soon as the law permitted and became naturalized in 1949. He joined the Democratic Party, was elected judge in the court of Westmoreland Judicial District, and served there until 1957.

When Saund ran for Congress in 1956, victory seemed unlikely. He was asked why he didn't join the local church and "get rid of this Hindu talk," but Saund said firmly that he would not change his Sikh religion: "No. I am what I am and I will not be a sham." His honesty and straightforwardness won over the voters, who elected him by a margin of more than 4,000 votes.

As a freshman congressman, he was given the rare honor of an appointment to the powerful House Committee on Foreign Relations and asked to tour India to study the effectiveness of the government's foreign-aid program. He was going to visit his homeland after having been away for 37 years and was apprehensive, because, in his words, he had "renounced my Indian birthright for American citizenship. Would I be welcomed or booed?" His fears were unfounded. He was welcomed warmly everywhere he went, especially in his native village. Throughout his travels, he presented himself as "a living example of American democracy." On his return to the United States, he spoke of his tour in glowing terms, "The thrilling fact is that throughout Asia, and especially in India, the people hold America in such great esteem, they are proud that one of [their own] has been freely elected to the United States Congress."*

On June 29, 2005, the U.S. Senate voted unanimously to honor Saund by naming the U.S. Post Office at 30777 Rancho California Road in Temecula, California, in his honor, with the words, "The Dalip Singh Saund Post Office Building will honor an American who followed his dream to the United States, broke barriers, and served as a representative of the people. This Act of the Congress will preserve Congressman Saund's legacy and honor the success of all immigrants from India and their accomplishments."**

More than 40 years passed before another Indian American, Bobby Jindal, was elected to the U.S. House of Representatives from the First Congressional District of the state of Louisiana in 2004.

---

*Padma Rangaswamy, "Dalip Singh Saund," in *Asian American Encyclopedia* (Pasadena, Calif.: Salem Press, 1995).

**Indian Reporter*, July 15, 2005, 33.

Many Sikhs settled in California, where they established gurdwaras, or temples, including this one in Stockton, California, founded in 1912. In addition to serving as a house of worship, the gurdwara was also a place where Sikhs could gather and socialize among themselves.

(continued from page 27)

gain the right to full U.S. citizenship, including the right to own property and to marry whomever they choose. In Canada, Sikh pioneers fought steadfastly to establish rights and freedoms for their community and become integrated into Canadian society.

Despite all the hardships, Indians were able to create a supportive environment. The most important institution for the Sikhs was the *gurdwara*, or temple. The gurdwaras the Sikhs built in Stockton, Yuba City, Los Angeles, and other cities in California, as well as in and around Vancouver, British Columbia, in Canada, were more than places of religious worship. They served as shelters for elderly Sikh men, charitable houses to help the needy, and places where Sikhs could gather and socialize among themselves. They also enabled Sikh families to observe traditional last rites in accordance with the wishes of the deceased.

Among the early pioneers were also those who lived very different lives from the Sikh farmers. Gobind Behari Lal (1889–1982) was a Pulitzer Prize–winning science journalist who had a long and distinguished career as a science editor, working in San Francisco, New York, and Los Angeles. He traveled widely, lectured around the world, and is best known for his contribution to popularizing science among laypeople through his articles.[16]

YEARNINGS FOR THE HOMELAND

Although Indians were making a life for themselves in the United States, they did not forget their families back home. Many of them had left behind wives and children, and they sent money home regularly to support them. They also sympathized with India's struggle for independence from British rule and actively campaigned in the United States for India's freedom. The most well known among these early activists was Taraknath Das, who published a newspaper called *Free Hindustan* and founded a society called "Friends of Freedom." Another intellectual, Lala Har Dayal, gave up a British government scholarship at Oxford University and taught at Stanford before becoming a revolutionary.

Under their leadership, Indians came together to collect funds, distribute literature, and form a political party called *Ghadr*, meaning "revolutionary" in Arabic. A group of them even set sail from San Francisco to Calcutta (now called Kolkata) in 1914, hoping to start a revolution, but their leaders were arrested in India, and the movement quickly collapsed. The Indians had believed that, because it had also been a former British colony and fought its own bloody war of independence from Great Britain, the United States would support their revolutionary activities. But strong ties between the United States and England ensured that Indians, far from being encouraged in their struggle, were caught and jailed for their activities.

| Number of Immigrants Admitted to the United States from India, 1820–1960 ||
Year of Entry	Number Admitted
1820	1
1821–1830	8
1831–1840	39
1841–1850	36
1851–1860	43
1861–1870	69
1871–1880	163
1881–1890	269
1891–1900	68
1901–1910	4,713
1911–1920	2,082
1921–1930	1,886
1931–1940	496
1941–1950	1,761
1951–1960	1,973

In 1921, the U.S. Congress passed the racist "quota law," which limited new immigration to 3 percent of the number of persons of each nationality already in the United States according to the 1910 U.S. census. Realizing that many southern and eastern Europeans had already entered the United States by this time, and wanting to keep them out, Congress changed the law in 1924. They restricted the quota to 2 percent and based it on the 1890 U.S. census, when most Americans were still whites from northern and western Europe. This law excluded *all* Asians, including Indians, who were already shut out by the Barred Zone Act of 1917.

By the time India gained its independence from Great Britain in 1947, the United States had become a world power and began to reconsider some of its own restrictive immigration laws. In 1946, it granted India a quota of 100 immigrants per year, and a gradual trickle of legal immigration, mainly families of those already in the United States and some university students, began and continued through the 1950s and 1960s.

In 1965, President Lyndon B. Johnson reformed immigration law so that, for the very first time in U.S. history, race was dropped as a basis for immigration and a system based on quotas was adopted for each country. A limit of 20,000 immigrants per country was set, and India was among them. Preferences were given to professionals and the immediate family members of U.S. citizens and permanent residents. Indians began to arrive in record numbers, creating a new community of immigrants very different from the old group.

• Study Questions •

1. What part of India did the early Indian immigrants come from? What religion did they belong to?

2. Why did they leave home?

3. How were they received in North America? Who was against them and why?

4. Identify at least three specific barriers faced by the early Asian immigrants.

5. What strategies did Indian immigrants use to overcome these barriers?

6. What connections did they maintain with the homeland?

7. Who is Dalip Singh Saund? How do you account for his rise to high office?

8. When and why did Indians stop immigrating to the United States?

3

Democratic India:

A Wondrous Blend of Ancient and Modern

Much can be said about Indian culture and how it affects the Indian view of democracy. U.S. President William J. Clinton made such observations when he addressed the Indian Parliament during his visit to India on March 22, 2000:

> Here is a country where more than 2 million people hold elected office in local government; a country that shows at every election that those who possess the least cherish their vote the most. Far from washing away the uniqueness of your culture, your democracy has brought out the richness of its tapestry, and given you the knot that holds it together.

As the world's most populous democracy and a major supplier of technological talent to the world, India has gained a reputation as an "emerging power." It is also home to the largest number of poor people, however, and one of the world's most ancient civilizations. Finally, it is a nuclear nation that embraces peace and nonviolence. The contradictions and paradoxes of India are a product of 5,000 years of history. Over the years, foreign conquerors have brought new influences of religion, art, architecture, politics, and culture, all of which have been absorbed and are reflected in the India of today. Dramatic changes are taking place in India as it undergoes economic and social transformation.

DIVERSITY AND DEMOCRACY

India is a peninsula, a rough triangle bounded on the north by the world's highest mountain range, the Himalayas (which means "abode of snow"), and surrounded on the other two sides by water. Its physical landscape varies from the barren dunes of the Thar Desert to the tropical forests of the rain-drenched northeast. Several major rivers, including the Ganges, Brahmaputra, and Indus, are fed by the melting snow and ice of the northern mountains. They carry rich soil to the plains below, where they have supported agriculture-based civilizations for thousands of years. Throughout India's history, traders and armies have penetrated its borders, either through passes in the northwest mountain ranges of the Hindu Kush, or by sea. In central India are the Vindhya Mountains, which act as a natural barrier between north and south. Rarely have empires crossed this barrier to bring all of India under one rule, so a variety of kingdoms have flourished at different times, giving India its rich historical diversity.

India is the world's seventh-largest country in area, occupying about 1.2 million square miles (3.2 million square kilometers). The country is home to 1.08 billion people, or about one-sixth of the world's population. (Only China has more people.) In comparison to the United States, India is one-third its size but has more than three times its population. (The U.S. population is estimated to be about 295 million.) More than half of India's land is suitable for growing crops, and about a fourth (or 25 percent) of the country's people are still involved in farming,

The Republic of India has a unique religious heritage: It is the birthplace of four of the world's major religions—Hinduism, Buddhism, Jainism, and Sikhism. In addition, India is home to the world's third-largest Muslim population. Here, Muslim devotees gather at the Jama-Masjid Mosque in New Delhi during the Muslim feast of Eid al-Adha.

compared to less than 1 percent in the United States. What India does have in common with the United States is its democratic system of government and the diversity of its people. Both countries tolerate difference and subscribe to the same ideal of equal opportunity for all.

The Republic of India (also known as *Bharat*) has 28 states and 7 union territories (smaller regions with special status.) Its capital is New Delhi, and the official language is Hindi, which is spoken by about 30 percent of the people, mostly in northern India. English has the status of an associate language and is the most important language for national, political, and commercial communication throughout India. There are 17 other official "scheduled" languages and more than 1,000 lesser languages and dialects spoken by a multitude of ethnic groups.[17]

Religious diversity in India is equally complex. India is the birthplace of four of the world's major religions: Hinduism, Buddhism, Jainism, and Sikhism, but another major religion, Islam, has more followers in India than any other country of the world, except Indonesia and Pakistan. Christianity came to India even before it spread to Europe. The Apostle Saint Thomas traveled to the southern coast of India to spread the gospel and was buried in Chennai in A.D. 70. About 2 percent of India's population is Christian.

India is the only country where Jews were welcomed and never persecuted (though most have immigrated to Israel), and where Zoroastrians, also known as Parsis, found refuge when they fled Muslim persecution in Persia in the seventh century A.D. In addition, millions of Indians still follow ancient tribal religions. For them, local spirits and deities are very much a part of their natural environment, and they worship them in the same way that their ancestors, the original inhabitants of India, did thousands of years ago.

ANCIENT ROOTS

Until recently, it was believed that Indian civilization started with raids by the Aryans from Central Asia around 1500 B.C., but an archaeological discovery in 1921 unearthed the remains of highly advanced towns and villages in Mohenjo-daro and Harappa in the Punjab that appear to have existed between 3000 and 1700 B.C. Aryans brought with them the Sanskrit language, the Hindu religion, and the caste system, all of which form the basis of classic Indian civilization. They built great cities in northern India and wrote the sacred Hindu texts of the *Vedas* and composed the epics *Mahabharata* and *Ramayana*. These stories are enacted in festivals throughout India to this day.

The Aryans formalized the rituals and practices of Hinduism, which include the belief in the oneness of the individual soul and the Supreme Divine Being (*Brahman*), and the cycle of birth and rebirth. As in many other religions, Hindus believe that after the death of the body, the immortal soul is reborn into a life that is better or worse, depending on one's good or bad actions (*karma*). Those who follow the right path and perform their righteous duty (*dharma*) may achieve liberation (*moksha*) from the cycle of birth and rebirth, and attain eternal bliss (*nirvana*) or union with Brahman.[18]

Hinduism has no single historical founder or central authority, nor is it an organized religion, where worshippers may follow a prescribed set of rules laid down by holy books (such as the Ten Commandments of Christianity or the Five Pillars [principal tenets] of Islam). There is no required attendance at a house of worship in order to prove the faith. The many gods and goddesses of Hinduism represent many concrete forms of a single universal reality. This openness and tolerance is Hinduism's greatest strength and has enabled it to survive the many challenges it has faced throughout history. More than 80 percent of India's population is Hindu, making it the dominant religion of the land.

Another important aspect of Hinduism is the caste system, a social hierarchy used until recently that reflected four broad occupational groupings. At the very top were *Brahmins* (different from *Brahman*, the Supreme Being), the priests and scholars. Then came *Kshatriyas*, the warrior or soldier class (kings belonged to this category). The third group were *Vaisyas,* or the merchant class, followed by *Sudras*, or peasant workers. Outside the caste system entirely were the *Untouchables*, who performed "polluting" jobs such as disposing of human waste and cremating the dead.

People were born into a particular caste, and they were expected to marry within the caste and perform their duty according to their station in life. Though the caste system was most pronounced among Hindus, it spread across all religious groups and social classes in India. No matter what purpose it served, the fundamental inequality of the caste system was continuously challenged throughout India's history. Mahatma Gandhi, who led India's independence movement against the British, called for abolishing the system. In modern India, the government has a policy of giving the lower castes special privileges, similar to the affirmative action policy of the United States, to make up for discrimination suffered in the past by members of lower castes.

Two of the earliest challenges to Hinduism came from Gautama Buddha (born in 563 B.C.), founder of the Buddhist religion, and Mahavira (born in 599 B.C.), founder of the Jain religion. They rejected the rituals of the Vedas and the tyranny of the caste system. Buddha stressed the importance of moderation and the middle path as an end to suffering, whereas Jains saw nonviolence to all living beings as a guiding principle. Neither of these religions gained importance over Hinduism; rather, Hinduism absorbed their beliefs and evolved into newer and more popular forms. It was also about this time (more than 2,500 years ago) that the first emigrants from India traveled to foreign lands, carrying the message of Buddha to countries in the Far East, where Buddhism took root and flourished.

REGIONAL INFLUENCES

The early dynasties that ruled India were mostly Hindu. King Asoka of the Mauryan Dynasty (third century B.C.) was the first to create a large Indian empire. Islam came to India both by sea and by land, brought by Arab traders to the west coast of Gujarat in the seventh century A.D. and also by Turkish and Afghan armies, who came through the Khyber Pass and established rule over parts of northern India in the eleventh and twelfth centuries. The Mughal Empire was founded in India in the sixteenth century by Babur, a descendant of the Turk Tamerlane and the Mongol Genghis Khan. Babur established a dynasty that lasted nearly 300 years. Dance and music, poetry, painting, art, and architecture flourished in a blend of Hindu and Muslim culture, as a succession of Mughal emperors entered into alliances, conquered new territories, and expanded their empire. Among them was Emperor Shah Jehan, who built the famous Taj Mahal in Agra.

In southern India, early Hindu dynasties built flourishing temple cities, and as early as the sixth century A.D. spread Hinduism eastward to the countries of Thailand, Malaysia, Cambodia, and Indonesia. In central India, in the Deccan Plateau, Muslim kingdoms established themselves through military conquest. Many indigenous people converted to Islam and the Muslim population of India increased significantly. By the end

The Mughal Dynasty ruled India from the early sixteenth century to the mid-eighteenth century. Among its more prominent rulers was Shah Jehan, who reigned from 1628 to 1658 and built one of the world's most famous structures, the Taj Mahal, located near Agra, in north-central India.

of the eighteenth century, Mughal power declined, as regional kingdoms established their independence and the Europeans entered the scene.

COLONIZED BY THE BRITISH

The arrival of the Europeans in India was heralded by the Portuguese explorer Vasco da Gama, who landed in Goa on India's west coast in 1498. He was followed by Dutch, French, and British private trading companies. The British East India Company started off as a commercial enterprise but soon became involved in Mughal military conflicts. They ousted the French and gradually wrested control of much of India from the Mughals. The Indians, straining under the domination of the British, revolted against them in the First War of Independence in 1857. The rebellion was crushed with brutal force, and after that, the British Crown took over and India became a colony of Great Britain.[19]

It was under the British that the first large-scale emigration took place from India to many parts of the globe. In 1834, Britain abolished the slave trade and began to ship thousands of indentured Indian laborers to replace the freed African slaves in the sugar and rice plantations of the Caribbean and Pacific colonies, and east and south Africa. Indenture is a form of bonded labor where a worker contracts with an employer to serve for a fixed period of time in return for free passage and basic food, accommodation, and medical care.

The conditions of indenture were often worse than slavery, however, and Indians suffered a great deal under this system. A total of 1.5 million Indians were shipped to other places between 1834 and 1917. About two-thirds of those who went abroad as indentured labor never returned to India, and their descendants now form sizeable populations of Indians in all these countries. Many of the descendants migrated in the late twentieth century to the industrialized countries of Europe, and to Canada and the United States. Indians were also sent

Mahatma Gandhi—pictured here with Manibehn Patel, the daughter of Indian political leader Vithalbhai Patel— was a key figure in the Indian independence movement. Gandhi advocated satyagraha—the promotion of political and social reform through peaceful civil disobedience.

to work as middle-level administrative officers for the British government in Burma (now Myanmar), Malaya (now Malaysia), and East Africa. Still others went as free merchants to these colonies.[20]

The 200 or so years of British rule represent a mixed bag for India. Britain exploited India's natural and human resources, kept its economy suppressed, and denied Indians their basic civil rights. On the other hand, they also created an administrative network that included a vast education system and communication facilities in the form of seaports, post offices, and railways, which brought India into the modern era. The British left India as the result of a long struggle for independence led by Mahatma Gandhi, who became world famous as the apostle of peace and nonviolence. Gandhi's tactic of civil disobedience (not obeying a law that was morally wrong) was successfully adopted by Martin Luther King, Jr. during the American civil rights movement of the 1960s.

INDEPENDENT INDIA

When the British left India in 1947, they divided the country into two nations, India and Muslim Pakistan. Millions were killed or wounded as Hindus and Muslims crossed the border in the violent conflict of partition. Both countries laid claim to the state of Kashmir and have fought two wars over it since independence, but the dispute is still unresolved. Pakistan became a Muslim state, whereas India chose the path of secularism, meaning that the government does not support one religion over another but encourages all religions to flourish. India's constitution, which took its inspiration from the U.S. constitution, guarantees equal rights for all, regardless of caste, creed, gender, or religion. It has more than 200 political parties and one of the highest voter turnouts (more than 60 percent) in the world. Both the president and prime minister of India, who hold elected office, belong to small minority communities. The President, Dr. A. P. J. Abdul Kalam, is a Muslim (only about 13 percent of India is Muslim) and the prime minister, Dr. Manmohan Singh, is a Sikh (Sikhs make up about 2 percent of India's population).

After India gained independence, large numbers of Indians immigrated to England in the 1950s and 1960s, and later, to

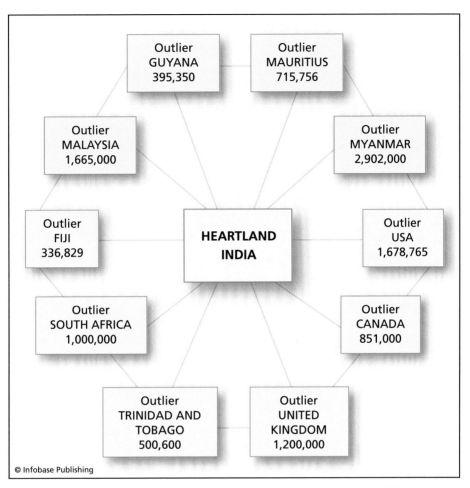

Outlier GUYANA 395,350	Outlier MAURITIUS 715,756	
Outlier MALAYSIA 1,665,000		Outlier MYANMAR 2,902,000
Outlier FIJI 336,829	HEARTLAND INDIA	Outlier USA 1,678,765
Outlier SOUTH AFRICA 1,000,000		Outlier CANADA 851,000
Outlier TRINIDAD AND TOBAGO 500,600	Outlier UNITED KINGDOM 1,200,000	

© Infobase Publishing

As this diagram illustrates, Indians live throughout the world, with the highest populations in Myanmar and the United States.

other Commonwealth countries such as Canada and Australia. No matter what part of the world they have immigrated to, Indians (called NRIs or Nonresident Indians) remain in touch with India and with Indians elsewhere in a global network called the *oikumene*. An oikumene is a household (from the Greek word *oikos*, meaning "home") whose members are connected by ties of family, religion, trade, profession, and culture.

The second half of the twentieth century was a period of nation-building for India. Led by its first prime minister,

Jawaharlal Nehru, and later by his daughter, prime minister Indira Gandhi, India adopted a socialist path where the government was heavily involved in planning the economy. It was during this period that many educated Indians, unable to find jobs, immigrated to Canada and the United States. In the 1990s, however, India opened up its markets, many government controls were lifted, and the economy grew rapidly.

India now has the world's largest middle class, more than 300 million strong, with an appetite for consumer goods. India is also attracting investment in different sectors, such as road-building, energy, aviation, and telecommunications. In 2003, there were more than 26 million cell phones in India, a sign of rapid growth, though still a far cry from the U.S. figure of 158 million.[21]

More and more companies in Europe and North America are hiring people in India to do their office work through a process known as "outsourcing." Indians have strong technical skills, speak fluent English, and can do the work for less money. Because of the time difference, they can also help increase production (Indians can work by day while it is nighttime in the United States.) This kind of information-technology work earned India $17 billion in 2004 and has exceeded $22 billion in 2005.[22] Multinational companies such as Pepsico, Motorola, IBM, Ford, and Microsoft run operations in India. Although some Indians welcome their presence, others see them as bringing in too much Westernization, making the rich richer but not helping to remove widespread poverty.

India faces many challenges in the twenty-first century. About a quarter of its population lives below the poverty line, its per-capita income is only around $3,000 (compared to $40,000 in the United States), and only 60 percent of its population is literate (compared to 97 percent in the United States).[23] It is obvious that India has a long way to go to catch up with the developed nations, but it has stood steadfast in the path it has chosen to economic progress, as well as to its commitment to democracy and religious pluralism.

• Study Questions •

1. How does India compare with the United States in the following areas: size, population, farming sector, literacy, cell-phone usage, and per-capita income? What are the implications of these disparities?

2. What do the United States and India have in common?

3. When did the Aryans come to India? From where? How did they influence India?

4. Identify some basic characteristics of the Hindu religion. How does it compare with Christianity and Islam? What other religions are practiced in India?

5. What is the caste system? What is its relevance in modern India?

6. Who were the Mughals? Who built the Taj Mahal?

7. What is indenture? Which countries were affected by it and how?

8. What legacy did the British leave behind in India?

9. Name some of the founding principles of independent India.

10. Define outsourcing. What are its benefits and drawbacks?

4

Why Leave Home for America?

After India gained its independence in 1947, a new era began. Indians were allowed to become U.S. citizens, and more and more students were admitted to American universities. Things changed even more dramatically after the immigration laws were reformed in 1965. The new laws actively encouraged emigration from India, even though it was still highly selective. Under an elaborate system, preference was given to skilled professionals who were in short supply in the United States, such as doctors and nurses, engineers, and scientists. The shortage was caused by many factors: Young Americans were away fighting the Vietnam War and the United States was in a race with the Soviet Union to land a man on the moon, which created a demand for scientists and engineers. Expanded hospital services in new social programs such as Medicare and Medicaid created a need for doctors and nurses.

After the Immigration and Naturalization Services Act was passed in 1965, skilled Indian professionals, such as doctors and nurses, engineers, and scientists, were encouraged to immigrate to the United States. Pictured here is Dr. Jatin Shah, a world-renowned head and neck cancer surgeon at Sloan-Kettering Cancer Center in New York.

Between 1965 and 1980, about 175,000 Indians, most of them professionals, immigrated to the United States.[24] They settled in metropolitan areas, where professional jobs were readily available in factories, hospitals, and universities. At the same time, educated and urbanized Indians started to immigrate to Canada under liberalized immigration laws there, increasing their population from around 7,000 in 1968 to more than 850,000 by the year 2000. Ninety percent of Canadian Indians live in the metropolitan areas of Toronto, Vancouver, Montreal, Calgary, and Edmonton.

SPIRIT OF ADVENTURE

What were the conditions in the home country that caused Indians to migrate in such large numbers? In the 1960s, India had a large pool of young highly skilled professionals who were educated in the schools left behind by the British. They spoke excellent English and were familiar with Western systems but were unemployed because the Indian economy was not growing fast enough to provide jobs for them. They learned about the United States from their relatives, who had visited abroad, and from recruiters, who told them of career opportunities. Many Indians came in a spirit of adventure, excited at the thought of staying a few years and returning home, not fully aware of how the journey might change their lives. In the words of one immigrant, "When we came here, we came as a batch of medical students. So it really wasn't a conscious decision. It didn't strike me at that time, what we were doing."[25] One mother, in a letter dated May 29, 1974, wrote to her cardiologist son in the Chicago area, "So my little Unni is now a great cardiologist! How happy and proud I am! . . . I suppose this qualification is enough to hold the highest position in this sub-specialty in any teaching institution. When you come home after a few months you must make a good probe and see if you can get into any ... such institutions in our own country."[26] Like the Sikh sojourners of the early twentieth century, many of these immigrants did not return to India except to visit. They stayed on to make America their home.

Unlike the early immigrants, however, most of the new immigrants were upper-class, urban professionals. They were not fleeing dire poverty or political persecution; rather, they came in the hopes of furthering their education and for economic and professional advancement. Some immigrants came alone, as bachelors, sharing an apartment with several other Indians, until they could afford their own place and send for their families. Sometimes, it was a single woman who came on her own. In the words of one woman immigrant from Delhi,

> This was 1976 and I had to make a decision whether to go back to India after my studies or stay on. I was single and getting older. It was a difficult decision, there were so many issues to be considered. . . . I missed the family, I missed Indian culture. At times I thought I would be better off with my family in India. I felt like I was betraying a country in which I had grown up. I had been very happy, very contented, had very good friends in India. . . . But there is always ambivalence. One can always think back and say, "What would have happened had I gone back?" I think there are always questions that are open.[27]

Other women came with their husbands, like this well-educated woman whose family was already part of the oikumene:

> I was born in Himachal Pradesh, lived all my life in Delhi, did my Master's in Delhi University and got married at twenty-two. I saw my husband only after the wedding. He was doing his residency in Lucknow. We stayed there three years while he finished and then we came to England. My side of the family has been living in America and England for many years since the 1950s. England was only a means to come to America. Even in India, this is where we wanted to come eventually.[28]

Almost half of the 584,302 immigrants who emigrated from India to the United States between 1965 and 1993 were women. This female population was extremely important in helping Indian Americans form a successful community, with stable families, and was a sharp contrast to the earlier Sikh immigration, where the women were left behind.

Emigration from India was not usually an individual decision. In a culture where family ties and duty to elders is considered very important, the young immigrant had to weigh several factors. Who would care for the elderly parents who might be left behind? Who would mind the

First-Person Account

BRAIN DRAIN OR BRAIN GAIN?

In *A Patchwork Shawl: Chronicles of South Asian Women in America*, Sonia Shah, an investigative journalist and author whose work has appeared in such magazines as *The Nation* and *Salon* is one of several essayists who recount their experiences as women of South Asian descent in the United States. In the following excerpt, Shah explains why her parents immigrated to the United States:

Why did she, and my father, want to leave India? Then, as now, emigrating to the United States was considered a path to certain upward mobility. It was and is possible for elites to accumulate much wealth in India. But Indian immigrants to the United States consistently cite economic-related reasons for leaving: corruption, poverty, lack of opportunity. For example, when my mother graduated from medical school in the late 1960s, the postcolonial Indian economy suffered a surplus of educated labor. India's educated and unemployed numbered 1.53 million in 1969, and 3.3 million in 1972.

The [revised immigration laws of 1965], which abolished national quotas in favor of those based on professional status, aimed to encourage the immigration of such professionals. Thousands of unemployed professionals from India and Pakistan flocked to the United States, my parents among them. Medical graduates, especially, were encouraged, with offers of free apartments and secure jobs at hospitals. *

---

* Sonia Shah, "Three Hot Meals and a Full Day at Work," in Shamita Das Gupta, ed., *A Patchwork Shawl: Chronicles of South Asian Women in America* (New Brunswick, N.J.: Rutgers University Press, 1998), 208–210.

family business? Sometimes the eldest son was sent abroad, so he could become prosperous and send money home to support the others. The 1965 law allowed immigrants to sponsor family members, so as soon as they were well established (which happened very quickly, because they were well qualified and landed good jobs), they sent for their brothers and sisters.

OCCUPATIONAL VS. RELATIVES CATEGORIES

The early phase of immigration included the year 1975, when the U.S. Immigration Service classified 93 percent of Indian immigrants as "professional/technical workers" or as their spouses or children. Between 1980 and 1990, however, the majority of Indian immigrants were admitted, not under the "occupational," but under the "relatives" category. The Indian-American population thus grew from a primary group of professional immigrants to a more varied group of nonprofessional family members. This process of chain migration sometimes resulted in one primary immigrant bringing over as many as 19 other family members.[29]

Even when Indians were sponsored by other family members, they felt the uncertainties that are an unavoidable part of the immigrant experience, as told in this story of a woman who was sponsored by her husband's brother:

> We were middle class, not very high. We always aspired to be more. The idea of coming to the U.S. had been there ever since we got married in 1976. My husband wanted to study here, do his post-doc, but he realized he could not get into the U.S. except by immigration. My brother got his citizenship in 1981, sponsoring us took seven to eight years, and we finally got here in March 1989. . . . I can never forget the moment when the four of us—my husband and my two boys and me—got down in Chicago with a bag in our hands. The past was haunting us, the

future was totally a question mark. We felt so lonely, it was a turning point. A major change could also have happened in India, but being here and without family, in a new culture, it definitely added to the experience.[30]

For Indians, family is much more than the immediate, nuclear family. It is an extended network that includes a wide circle of relatives, and in subsequent years, Indian Americans brought over more and more family members, including their elderly parents. Unlike the United States and Canada, India lacks a Social Security system, so adults are primarily responsible for taking care of their parents in their old age. Some parents came willingly; others felt they had no choice, as illustrated in the following comments, from elderly immigrants. One was eager to come: "I wanted to come here in 1952 for further studies. I couldn't come then. Then I got a chance to send my son here for further education. I came here to enjoy my life with him. It was my own desire to understand America."[31] The other was more apprehensive:

> My coming here was not my personal decision. My children grew up and came abroad. I retired and my son asked me to join him here in the U.S. I said, "Let me first build my own house in India. What if I don't like it in your town? Where will I go?"... I also have a daughter in Houston. I feel that for my children, this country is better, atmosphere is healthier, but I also have attachments to India.[32]

Between 1980 and 1993, one in five Indian immigrants to the United States was over 50 years old.[33] As a result, within a short span of 30 or so years, there were three generations of Indian Americans in the United States—the immigrants, their parents, and their children. This helped make the community even more stable and diverse; it also gave families the opportunity to preserve their heritage and to benefit from the wisdom of their elders.

A GLOBAL MIGRATION

Some Indians came, not directly from India, but from former British colonies in Africa and the Caribbean and Pacific Islands. They were descendants of earlier immigrants who had been sent to those locations by the British. When these countries became independent in the 1960s, they struggled with poverty and unstable governments. Indians were caught in the middle of racial strife in places like Jamaica and Trinidad and Tobago, and many decided to immigrate to North America. Known as Indo-Caribbeans, they form a large and distinct population, both in Canada and the United States, especially in New York. Indians also fled Fiji, where they suffered political persecution from Fijians and feared for their lives and their property.

In the East African countries of Uganda, Kenya, and Tanzania, the descendants of indentured Indians were forced to leave, despite being prosperous, because the newly independent Africans resented them. In Uganda, for instance, in 1972, the dictator Idi Amin expelled all Indians, accusing them of not sharing their prosperity and not assimilating with the Africans. These East African Indians, most of them Gujarati, settled in England, Canada, and the United States but maintained a separate identity. "Indian Gujaratis would hear us speak and immediately tell we were not directly from Gujarat, that we were from East Africa," said one immigrant. "At every Indian gathering, I found myself seeking out and gravitating towards Indians from East Africa." Some East African Indians felt superior, because they were prosperous in Africa, and emigrated not for economic betterment like the Indians from India, but for political reasons. "We are also more well-traveled than the average Gujarati from India. Our horizons have expanded because we have moved in international circles. We are equally comfortable with Africans and whites, and don't have the same prejudices as the Indians from Gujarat. Also, many of us have had a more comfortable life."[34]

One type of immigration that isn't discussed much in the Indian-American community is illegal or undocumented immigration. Though it is a far smaller problem among Indian Americans than it is among other immigrant groups, such as Mexicans or Chinese, it does exist. Many Indians, particularly from the impoverished villages of Gujarat, pay astronomical fees to "agents" who smuggle them in and find them jobs in the service business, in restaurants or motels, where they are exploited.[35] Unable to discuss their plight for fear of being discovered, such immigrants remain part of the silent underground in many immigrant populations.

THE "IT" IMMIGRANTS

As the number of sponsored immigrants grew, their patterns of settlement changed. Instead of first coming to the cities and settling in transient neighborhoods, they went straight to their relatives, who had settled in the suburbs. Also, by the 1980s, many manufacturing jobs had moved from the major cities to the suburbs. Suburbs were also considered more desirable by Indians for their safe environments and better schools. In later years, manufacturing jobs were shifted to countries overseas, and new jobs were created in the United States.

In the 1990s, the United States entered the information age, when computers and information technology created a new demand for a different type of Information Technology or IT worker—the software engineer and the computer programmer. At the same time, India shifted from a closed, inward-looking, protectionist economy to a more open, liberalized, and global economy. It began to pay attention to the skills that were most in demand worldwide. Realizing that there would be a huge need for information-technology professionals, the Indian education system geared itself to producing computer experts. Soon, the number of Indians being admitted to the United States under "Employment-based Preferences" grew much more rapidly than the number sponsored by relatives. Thousands of Indians were admitted under a special H1B visa, which brought in computer professionals and allowed them to become permanent U.S. residents after working here for six years. Of all the countries that took advantage of this new need in the U.S. labor market, India ranked the highest. In 2004, India sent 83,502 workers, more than 25 percent of the total, under the category "Workers with Specialty Occupations."[36]

Indian Immigrants Admitted Under Different Preference Categories, 1998 to 2004

Year	Total	Family-sponsored preferences	Employment-based preferences	Immediate relatives of U.S. citizens (Total)	Spouses of U.S. citizens	Children	Parents
2004	70,116	13,307	38,443	16,942	9,051	1,292	6,599
2003	50,372	15,359	20,560	12,693	6,314	1,137	5,242
2002	71,105	11,402	42,885	15,077	7,601	1,138	6,338
2001	70,290	15,443	39,010	14,714	7,631	1,325	5,758
2000	42,046	14,267	15,557	11,543	5,645	1,267	4,631
1999	30,237	15,179	5,362	9,356	3,852	1,243	4,261
1998	6,482	15,375	9,533	11,058	4,348	1,357	5,353

Source: Department of Homeland Security Web site. Available online at http://www.uscis.gov/graphics/shared/statistics/yearbook/2004/table2.xls

A CHANGED ATMOSPHERE

In the twenty-first century, two major developments started to influence emigration from India. One was the September 11, 2001, terrorist attacks, which caused the United States to tighten immigration laws. All South Asians, regardless of their religion, found themselves targeted and treated with suspicion. More and more Indians who might have wanted to immigrate preferred to stay home. They could afford to do so now, because the job market at home had improved greatly with globalization. American and European companies were setting up offices in India and hiring Indians to do the very work that they

Many U.S. companies now have call centers in India, where operators are trained in English and American slang. Pictured here are operators at Wipro Spectramind, an outsourcing center in New Delhi.

were earlier giving to immigrants in their own countries, and the Indians were doing it at a much lower cost. India continued to send students and specialty workers to the United States even after 2001, but the trend might have continued to increase had not opportunities at home increased dramatically.

Emigration from India to the United States has always been a supply-and-demand equation. When the lumber-mill owners and railroad corporations of the Pacific Northwest needed cheap labor in the 1900s, Indian immigrants answered the call. One hundred years later, Indian immigrants were still helping to build a new America, by answering America's call for high-tech employees. The pull of the United States remains strong for Indians in many countries of the globe, but for Indians in their rapidly developing homeland, there are now many attractive alternatives to immigration.

• Study Questions •

1. How do you account for the surge in Indian immigration after 1965? Identify global forces, conditions in India and the United States, and personal motivations.

2. In what way was immigration selective? In what way was it balanced?

3. What is "brain drain"? Do you think the migration of skilled professionals was good or bad for India? Give reasons for your answer.

4. From which countries other than India did Indians immigrate to the United States? Under what circumstances?

5. How do you define a *global economy*? How has it affected Indian immigration?

5

Rapid Growth, Exciting Change

When you see Indian Americans walking down the street in certain neighborhoods (sometimes called "Little Indias"), dressed in their traditional clothing (a *sari* or *salwar kameez* for women and a *kurta* for men), you may wonder how many of them there are and how they came to be concentrated in certain areas. How did so many Indian shops spring up along one street? When exactly did it happen? In order to understand what is happening in one little neighborhood, we need to look at the large global picture, as well.

HOW MANY?

If you are impressed by statistics, consider this: Indian Americans are among the fastest-growing groups in the United States. Since 1961, more than 1 million Indian immigrants have come to American shores, and the Indian-American population had exceeded the 2 million mark by the year 2005. In Canada, where

Number of Immigrants Admitted to the United States from India, 1961–2004	
Year of Entry	**Number Admitted**
1961–1970	27,189
1971–1980	164,134
1981–1990	250,786
1991–2000	363,060
2001–2004	245,409
Total number admitted since 1961	**1,050,578**

Source: Department of Homeland Security Web site. Available online at *http://www.uscis.gov/graphics/shared/statistics/year-book/2004/table2.xls*

the government identifies immigrant populations by their ethnic and linguistic makeup, Indians are counted as South Asians, who numbered more than 850,000 in 2001. Indians in North America thus make up more than 10 percent of Indians in the diaspora or outliers of the oikumene (See figure on page 45).

The U.S. census count of Indian Americans, and other ethnic groups in the United States, is complicated by the fact that there are many Americans of mixed-race descent. As Indian Americans intermarry with other Americans of different races, their children may identify with any part of their ethnic heritage. When they identify with their Indian heritage, they add greatly to the population numbers.

WHERE DO THEY LIVE?

The states with the largest Indian-American population are California, New York, New Jersey, Texas, and Illinois (See table on page 64.) Most Indian Americans are concentrated in the cities of New York, Philadelphia, Washington, D.C. (on the East Coast); Chicago (in the Midwest); and Los Angeles and San

Francisco (on the West Coast). Other cities such as Atlanta and Seattle are also attracting Indians in increasing numbers. The biggest increases between 1990 and 2000 occurred in southern states such as Georgia, North Carolina, and Tennessee. In Canada, the major concentrations of Indians are in Ontario (121,000) and British Columbia (74,000).[37]

Indians who arrived in the first wave of immigration after 1965 settled in the cities, but as they became more prosperous, they moved out to the suburbs. In New York, Indian professionals and students first lived in Manhattan but later moved to Queens and then farther out to predominantly white, affluent suburbs. In many states such as Illinois, certain suburbs came to be identified as heavily Indian (for example, Naperville, Skokie, and Des Plaines). Concentrations are heaviest in such New Jersey towns as Edison and Woodbridge, where Indians live in most neighborhoods. Millbourne, Pennsylvania, is the only town in the United States with a majority Indian population. Almost 63 percent of Millbourne's estimated population of 994 consists of Indians, mostly Sikhs.[38]

Even as the suburban population of Indian Americans was growing, the number of Indian Americans in the cities also increased. Newly arriving, unskilled relatives of Indian residents decided to open shops and restaurants, very often in the same neighborhoods in which Indians had originally settled. They developed these areas into commercial districts that provided ethnic goods and services to a growing population. Areas such as Devon Avenue in Chicago, Jackson Heights in New York, and Artesia in California came to be called "Little India," because of their clusters of ethnic businesses and residences.

The first businesses to spring up in the Indian community were the small grocery stores, which sold Indian goods, including spices and specialty foods. Then came the restaurants, which at first were popular with Indians but gradually came to be patronized by other Americans looking for variety in their dining experience. In the 1970s and 1980s, when Indians started to

Two Indian-American men walk down the street in the Devon Avenue section of northern Chicago. Today, there are more than 80,000 Indian-American residents in Chicago—the third-largest concentration in the United States.

return home for visits, stores sprang up that sold saris and electronic goods that were favorite gifts for relatives. By the 1990s, a new generation of Indians, born and bred in the United States, began to enjoy music and movies made in India, so a spate of video and music stores sprang up to cater to their needs. Boutiques selling fashionable Indian ethnic attire, *henna* salons (henna is a vegetable dye applied to the skin to create "temporary tattoos" popular at Indian weddings), and stores selling phone cards and satellite TV channels beamed from India

States with the Highest Population of Indian Americans, 2000	
State	**Indian-American Population**
California	314,819
New York	251,724
New Jersey	169,180
Texas	129,365
Illinois	124,723

all added to the exciting shopping experience. Generally, these stores were clustered in the Little Indias, but as the suburban population increased, Indian shopping complexes appeared in the suburbs, as well. Thus, the growth of the Indian community has created new jobs and new shopping and dining experiences for all Americans, and changed the face of neighborhoods all across the United States.

MAKING A LIVING

Indian Americans have consistently boasted the highest income of all ethnic groups in the United States. In 1999, their average household income was $63,669, much higher than the U.S. average of $41,994. Some Indians made enormous fortunes in the technology boom of the 1990s. Companies such as Microsoft, Apple, and Intel hired Indians by the thousands and fueled prosperity in the community. (On the flip side, many Indian Americans lost heavily in the technology bust after 2000, and still others lost their jobs to outsourcing and were forced to return home.) Among the more wealthy Indians were also engineers and scientists who worked in large corporations, then used their salaried earnings to start successful businesses.[39]

About 60 percent of Indian Americans are in management and professional occupations. Many leading, high-wage positions held by Indian Americans are in the medical professions. Nearly one in four Indian-American professionals and nearly one in five service providers is in the health-care industry. Other Indian Americans are employed in the financial services sector and by insurance, real estate, and travel agencies.

Indian Americans are also employed in many "niche" industries, meaning as a group they are concentrated in certain sectors, like Koreans in the dry-cleaning business or Vietnamese who run nail salons. As small business owners and operators, Indian Americans first became visible in the convenience store business, running White Hen pantries and 7-Eleven corner stores. Some became prosperous in the hotel/motel industry. Most hotel owners belong to the Patel community of Gujarat, and there are many amusing anecdotes in the community about the "Patel-hotel-motel" connection. Indians are also highly visible as newsstand operators in corner kiosks and subway stations, especially in New York, California, Pennsylvania, New Jersey, and Illinois. In the Midwest, an overwhelming majority (90 percent) of Dunkin' Donuts shops are owned, operated, or staffed by Indians and Pakistanis. Indians also bought into other franchises, such as Subway-sandwich and gas-station outlets. In many cases, these entrepreneurs started off with one or two units, brought in extended family members to strengthen and expand the business, and wound up as very wealthy owners of multiple units.

In contrast to the more successful, higher economic class of Indian Americans, there are thousands trapped in the lower sectors of the economy. They speak little English and have joined the blue-collar workforce as taxi drivers, backroom assistants in shops and restaurants, and factory workers. The community is thus faced with a widening gap between rich and poor.

THE VALUE OF EDUCATION

The wealth in the Indian-American population is not surprising, considering that Indian Americans have the highest educational levels of all Americans. Almost two-thirds (64 percent) of the adults have a bachelor's degree or higher, compared to about one-quarter (24 percent) of the U.S. population. More than one-third (34 percent) of Indian Americans have graduate or professional degrees, compared to less than one-tenth (9 percent) of the U.S. population. This is partly because of the selective nature of immigration laws, which, in the beginning, permitted only educated Indians and those with much-needed professional skills to enter the country. It is also because of the high value that Indian families place on education. Most Indian immigrant families invest first in acquiring the best education they can, for themselves and their children, before investing in a home or a business. At the same time, studies have shown that Indians, both men and women, are not always paid as highly as whites for the same work. Many have encountered a "glass ceiling," where they have been passed over for promotion because of their ethnicity. Others have struggled before achieving success, like this woman, who arrived in the 1980s:

> My husband was sure he would find work in America with his education and experience (with a pharmaceutical firm in India) but he wasn't getting a break. He had to pass some exams. I was fortunate to get a job within one month. My friends were not in the same position or in the same field to get me work. It just so happened I got my job through an Indian. But I am sure if I had been willing to work hard, put in eight hours at Jewel or McDonalds, I would still have managed.[40]

Like Indian men, Indian women are highly educated, and a large proportion of them can be found in professional and technical occupations. There is also an increasing number who have less than a fifth-grade education, however, especially among the newer arrivals. These women work out of the home, preparing packaged foods for sale in Indian grocery stores, or providing babysitting and domestic services. As workers in the "informal" or "unorganized" sectors of the economy, their work often remains unrecognized, underpaid, or even unpaid.

Dual-income households are common, and Indian boys and girls in the United States are equally encouraged to pursue higher education and secure good jobs. Despite the pressures to follow in their parents' footsteps as engineers or doctors, young Indian Americans are pursuing careers in nontraditional areas, such as the arts and entertainment, environmental activism, and social service, as in the case of this young Indian American:

> When my parents knew about my wanting to be an Education major, there was a huge rift. They forced—no, that's not the right word—they encouraged me very strongly to go into engineering. So I went down to Champaign to do engineering for a year and a half, but I didn't like the classes. I want to be a high school teacher. I got my degree and for these last few months I've been working in this low-income project with blacks and Hispanics. My parents see what I want to do and have come to terms with it.[41]

THE INDIAN-AMERICAN FAMILY

The 2000 U.S. census illustrated that the Indian-American population is much younger than the general U.S. population, with a median age of 30, compared to the U.S. median age of 35. More than two-thirds of the population consists of married people, and the divorce rate is very low—only one-fifth of that of all other Americans. The average family size is slightly larger than the American average, 3.5 compared to 3.1.

When the first immigrant couples had their children, many of them sent for their parents to help them with babysitting. In the 1970s and 1980s, the number of quality child-care facilities was inadequate, and the new immigrants preferred to raise their children at home, under the influence of their own culture, rather than outside in a new environment that they themselves were not yet used to. Consequently, Indian families, compared to other immigrant groups, had grandparents in their households at a fairly early stage.

The brothers and sisters that Indian-American immigrants sponsored later on often came with their own families, where children ranged in age from the very young to those nearing adulthood. Those who came as young children are called the "knee-high" or the "one-and-a-half" generation, because they see themselves as caught between the first generation of immigrants and the second generation of native-born Indian Americans. As the immigration of more young people continued in the 1990s, it created a healthy mix, adding to the complexity of the family structure among Indian immigrants.

In the Indian-American community, there are thus single young men and women, families with growing children, and "empty nesters" (whose children have grown up and left home), as well as senior citizens ready for retirement homes. They may live together as nuclear families, which includes just parents and children, or in households where many unrelated immigrants live together temporarily for economic reasons. Sometimes, the sponsored siblings live with the sponsoring family until they can afford to live on their own. A joint family in India often consists of several married family members living under the wing of their parents, contributing their income to the general household and sharing the resources. Such arrangements are also entered into by Indian Americans as immigration of relatives puts new demands on them. The general trend, however, is for Indian-American families to live in nuclear households, in keeping with the American norm.

The traditional family structure in India is still patriarchal, and the father is the ultimate authority figure in a household. Great respect is also given to elders in the family. Although these traditional values have enriched the lives of Indian-American families in many ways, they also have caused stress for those who have had to accommodate the needs of several relatives.

One Indian grandparent speaks of the changing relationships with her grandchildren:

> My grandchildren always want to know if I will be home when they come back from school. They say, "We don't like it when you go out. You aren't going out anywhere today are you?" But these children aren't as close to their parents as our children were to us. Maybe it is a generational thing. Each new generation is less attached to their parents. Children who are three, four, seven years old spend more time with their grandparents and are closer to them. But when they turn seventeen or nineteen and twenty, then it is different.[42]

The traditional Hindu wedding ceremony is still an important part of Indian-American culture in the United States. A young couple are pictured here receiving a wedding blessing from a Hindu priest, as their parents participate in the ceremony.

As young Indian Americans reach adulthood, one of the main concerns in the community is the issue of marriage. The tradition of arranged marriage, where the parents pick the bride or groom for their children, continues to be practiced in the United States, but in highly modified ways. Indeed, it takes such varied forms that the concept itself is not fully understood by

Tracing Your Roots

FAMILY NAMES REVEAL ORIGINS

In India, family names provide important clues about origin, and Indians themselves are able to "place" people based on their name, making an educated guess as to what part of India they are from, what language they speak, and even what caste and religion they belong to. Different regions of India follow different naming conventions. For instance, in southern India, a full name N. Subramaniam Iyer consists of an initial N. followed by the given name, Subramaniam, and the caste name, Iyer. (A single initial probably stands for the father's name, multiple initials may stand for the village of birth or the caste.)

When Mr. N. Subramaniam Iyer arrives as an immigrant to the United States, it may happen that his given name, Subramaniam, or his caste name, Iyer, becomes his last name. Such changes, of course, make tracing one's roots particularly difficult. One can guess, though, that Mr. Subramaniam is a Tamil-speaking Brahmin, probably from the state of Tamil Nadu in southern India. Other parts of India are more likely to follow the Western tradition of a given first name and family last name, such as Deepak Baneerjee or Rajiv Gupta.

Some last names, like Patel and Singh, are particularly common among Indian Americans. A Singh is usually Sikh (though there are Hindu Singhs from Bihar or Uttar Pradesh), whereas a Patel is Gujarati.

those outside the culture. An "arrangement" could consist of anything from an Indian American going back to India to marry someone chosen by his/her family—someone he/she may have met only a couple of times—to an Indian American merely being introduced to several "suitable" prospects, meaning those of the same socioeconomic, linguistic, and religious background.

The best way to trace one's family roots is to start with a blank family group record, using genealogy Web sites and family tree software. Start with yourself, list your siblings, and create separate branches for your father and mother. Depending on when your ancestors came to the United States, you might find detailed records about births, marriages, and deaths in U.S. county records, but if your parents were the first immigrants, chances are you will have to get your information from other sources. You may have to interview them and other family members. Ask them and other relatives, such as your grandparents, uncles, and cousins, to fill in the blanks.

Modern Indian immigrants have cosmopolitan origins in India and other parts of the world, and may have had intercaste and interregional marriages, not to speak of marriage to a person of another race or nationality. So be sure to double-check your facts and get more than one source for the same piece of information, whenever possible. On your visits to the home country, be sure to seek out old family photographs, letters, diaries, and other such documents that will help you create an authentic history. Keep your eyes and ears open at family gatherings, community picnics, religious celebrations, and other such events where Indian Americans gather to meet with extended family and friends. Don't be afraid to ask questions, as Indians are generally eager to talk about family connections. Develop your contacts through the Internet and e-mail, and exchange communication (including digital photographs) with distant relatives in far-flung parts of the world to create a comprehensive family tree.

However much parents might want their children to marry within their own community, Indian-American youth, brought up in a culture of freedom and independence, want to make their own choices.[43] Even as the choices available for marriage within the Indian-American community are growing with the increased population, there is a parallel trend of Indians marrying into the mainstream. Such interracial marriages are often conducted with two wedding ceremonies, for example, one Christian or Jewish and the other Hindu or Muslim.

In many respects, the continuously changing character of the Indian-American community has kept it vibrant and full of surprises. Some Indian Americans are highly acculturated and blend thoroughly into mainstream American life, whereas others are still isolated in ethnic enclaves and steeped in old traditions. Changes in American society and the U.S. economy affect the lives of Indian immigrants, determining where they settle, what jobs they take, and how prosperous they are. With emigration from India continuing at a swift pace, the community is also changed in subtle ways by new influences brought in from the home country.

• Study Questions •

1. What is an oikumene? Can you think of countries other than India that have immigrants scattered throughout the world?

2. Name the states with the largest Indian-American populations. Which provinces in Canada have the highest concentrations of Indian Canadians?

3. Why do you think they are concentrated in these areas?

4. When did commercial activity grow in the Indian-American community? Why did it happen at this time?
....

5. What are the diverse occupations of Indian Americans? What problems did they have finding work?
....

6. What is a joint family? What is a nuclear family?
....

7. How has "relatives-sponsored" immigration affected work and family life for Indian Americans?
....

8. What are some family values and traditions that Indian Americans cherish?
....

6

Proud to Be
Indian American

"Indian American scientist earns U.S. patent." "Indian banker makes his way to top of Citibank." "Indian earns 2005 Ellis Medal of Honor." "Indian appointed engineering college dean."

These headlines, from the Community Focus sections of newspapers in the Chicagoland Indian ethnic media, are fairly typical of the contents of other Indian ethnic newspapers nationwide. They are a key indicator of what Indians are most proud of, namely, their landmark achievements in various fields of endeavor. Indian scientists and engineers are responsible for some of the most innovative advancements in the computer industry, Indian physicists have pioneered scientific breakthroughs, and Indian academics have risen to the top of their professions as deans of leading business, science, and engineering schools.

At the community level, Indian Americans have infused fresh vitality into decaying city neighborhoods and transformed America's religious landscape by building intricately carved temples and other houses of worship. Indian Americans are also proud of their strong family values and their contributions to food, festivities, and fun in American life. By continuing to be a distinctive culture, they have enriched the United States in myriad ways and constantly challenged its commitment to democracy and diversity.

As with any immigrant group, the first few years are spent in trying to establish themselves in a new environment. In the very process of doing that, Indian Americans contributed to the building of the United States—from the early Sikh pioneers who worked the land, to the more recent Indians who staffed the hospitals and universities, laboratories and factories. There are innumerable instances of outstanding individual achievement by Indian Americans, such as Nobel laureates Subrahmanyam Chandrasekhar and Gobind Lal Khurana. (See Chapter 9 for more on these and other individuals of outstanding achievement.) They have also consciously created group identities, forming professional, cultural, religious, and social organizations that helped them mobilize their resources and enhance their achievements. It is through these organized efforts that they managed to retain their heritage, create new traditions, and become more fully involved in American life.

PRESERVING CULTURE

The first organizations formed by Indians, such as the India League of America (established in 1972), were broad in nature and included all Indians, regardless of what part of India they came from. The Association of Indians in America (1967), whose mission is to "preserve our Indian heritage and meet the American commitment," was responsible for helping secure minority status for Asian Indians in 1970 and a separate census category in the 1980 U.S. census. The National Federation of Indian American Associations (1980), considered the largest United States–based umbrella organization of Indians in America, is dedicated to promoting unity among Indian Americans. These

Dance is an important way for Indian Americans to preserve their culture, and many groups hold workshops to promote classical dance styles, such as *Bharatanatyam* and *Kathak*. Pictured here is Krithika Rajkumar (left) and Novni Vinod of the Hindu Temple Rhythms, performing at the Detroit Historical Museum during the East Indian Cultural Workshop.

early organizations helped Indians to establish a broad-based identity and to represent themselves to the wider population.

Over the years, the increased immigration of Indians from different parts of India spawned many regional and linguistic organizations. Different regional groups of Bengalis, Gujaratis, Tamils, Punjabis, Telugus, and others each formed their own associations. They celebrated their language, customs, food, music, and dance, in elaborate cultural events that drew attendees from throughout the Indian oikumene. There was a time in the mid-1980s when broad-minded Indian Americans agonized over the divisive and fragmenting effects of so many different organizations, but they came to accept them as a reality. Each regional and linguistic group fiercely guards and promotes its own culture in India, and since Indian immigrants reflect the diversity of the home country, it was perceived as a natural and inevitable development in the new land.

The value in these organizations lies in their ability to connect Indians to their culture and help them develop relationships with their home state in India. For instance, the Punjabi Cultural Association may host a reception for the Chief Minister of the State of Punjab when he is visiting the United States. Members may make financial investments in the home state, raise money for charities in Punjab, explain American values to their fellow Punjabis in India, and, of course, preserve the Punjabi culture for future generations of Americans.

When they need to act in concert with other Indian Americans, for instance, in marching in an Indian Independence Day parade, or when they need to join hands with other Americans in celebrating the Fourth of July, regional organizations are happy to do so, as well. Giving awards for individual accomplishments of their members and publicizing them for other Americans to recognize are also ways in which these and other Indian organizations serve the community. Far from becoming irrelevant, they have become revitalized with continued emigration from India and growing regional pride in the motherland.

NURTURING RELIGIOUS FAITH

For Indian Americans, one of the most important elements of their heritage is their religious faith. For many, religious activity is much more intense in their new country than it was in the homeland, where they took their religious identity for granted. In the early days of immigration, they met informally and conducted religious ceremonies in the basements of their homes, but as soon as their resources permitted it, they began to build elaborate houses of worship, some costing millions of dollars, where they could practice their faith and pass on the heritage to their children. Each state with major Indian populations has several temples, mosques, gurdwaras, and even churches, which Indian immigrants built to suit their religious practices.

What does it mean to be free to practice your own religion and learn about your religious heritage in a new land where you are a minority? A young Indian-American student describes how a Hindu religious school (called *Bala Vihar*) helped her learn more about her heritage:

> I became more confident and sure of myself. With a wealth of knowledge by my side, I felt strong. I stood up to my classmates and introduced them to my beliefs. To my surprise, they stopped mocking me, and instead, wanted to learn more. . . . I felt a sense of belonging, but not sameness, as though I were an individual piece adding color to the complete picture. I could fit in but still be different.[44]

Hindus, who form the majority religious group among Indian Americans, have built beautiful temples to their many gods and goddesses, including the Balaji Temple in Pittsburgh, Pennsylvania, the Rama Temple in Chicago, Illinois, and the Meenakshi Temple in Houston, Texas. The Council of Hindu Temples of North America lists more than 160 Hindu temples on its Web site.

Although the physical features may be an exact replica of Indian temples, the ways in which temples are used by Indian

Religion remains an important part of many Indian Americans' lives, which is reflected by the numerous temples, mosques, and gurdwaras in the United States. Pictured here is Hema Muralidharan, a Hindu worshipper who is lighting a candle at the Hindu Temple of Central Indiana, which was inaugurated in February 2006.

Americans are uniquely suited to their own needs, and they have evolved over the years to meet the needs of new generations. Young Indians receive not only religious instruction in

Sunday school, but also a chance to learn yoga, Indian languages, music, and dance. They even receive coaching for SAT exams! They celebrate national and religious holidays such as *Navratri* (nine days and nights of dancing and festivities), culminating in *Diwali*, a festival of lights and fireworks that is as significant for Indians as Christmas is for Americans. At the same time, Indian Americans joyously celebrate Halloween, Thanksgiving, Hanukkah, Christmas, and other such American festivals with the same enthusiasm that they bring to their own Indian holidays. Temple members also conduct outreach work, with soup kitchens and charity drives for the needy, and they educate other Americans about Hinduism.

SUPPORTING THE PROFESSIONALS

Cutting across religious lines, Indian Americans have formed professional organizations, especially when they felt discriminated against at work. The American Association of Physicians of Indian Origin (AAPI), for instance, was formed in 1982 to fight discrimination against foreign medical graduates who were forced to meet tougher licensing standards than domestic medical graduates. With a membership base of 35,000 physicians and 10,000 medical students and residents in 2004, AAPI has successfully lobbied for fair medical practices that have improved the lot of all medical practitioners, regardless of ethnic origin.[45]

So, too, with the Asian American Hotel Owners Association (AAHOA). AAHOA was formed in 1989 to champion the rights of hotel/motel owners who were being denied insurance or losing business to blatantly discriminatory practices.[46] Other advocacy groups were formed by Indians in engineering, nursing, law, and the pharmaceutical industry. These professional organizations served a dual purpose: They helped Indians secure rights for themselves, but they also helped improve lending practices, labor laws, and human services in American society.

Indians have achieved remarkable success in the United States as entrepreneurs, primarily in the information-technology sector but also in fields as varied as franchising, global manufacturing, insurance and health services, biotechnology, construction, retail, distribution, transportation, and real estate. Going well beyond the "mom and pop" establishments that provided goods and services to their own communities, they made significant contributions to the wider economy. The 2000 U.S. census showed that 61,398, or 11 percent, of Indian-American households had self-employed income in 1999, with an aggregate income of $2.9 billion. According to a business report, Indians started 778 Silicon Valley start-ups in 1998, generating a total of 16,598 jobs. *BusinessWeek* reported in 1998 that nearly 40 percent of Silicon Valley start-ups in the 1990s had at least one founder of Indian origin.[47]

These successes are all the more remarkable because in the beginning, Indians were refused loans by banks and were thought to lack leadership and management skills. As they proved themselves to be astute entrepreneurs, however, they gained the trust of investors. Most of the billionaire entrepreneurs are graduates of Indian Institutes of Technology (IITs), located in major cities in India and widely acknowledged as among the world's pre-eminent engineering schools. IIT graduates in the United States have given generously to their alma maters, creating partnerships with prestigious institutions such as the Massachusetts Institute of Technology (MIT) and Stanford University. They have also been instrumental in helping start an organization known for supporting Indian-American entrepreneurs through networking, mentoring, and education called The Indus Entrepreneurs (TiE). Started in 1992, it has grown to 40 chapters in 9 countries, with a membership of 8,000.[48] Indian-American entrepreneurs enjoy a reputation as one of the most successful business minority segments in the United States.

Indian Americans also have groups in India and the United States connect with one another. Multinational companies seeking access to India's growing markets have relied on Indian Americans to forge vital links. Physicians give back to India by volunteering in hospitals on periodic visits home. They also donate equipment and train Indian doctors on up-to-date medical practices. Medical organizations like the AAPI Charitable Foundation have set up charity clinics in India. Such exchanges have helped boost the image of Indian Americans in their homeland.

BREAKING NEW GROUND

The achievements of young Indian-American professionals lie not only in their having followed successfully in the paths laid out by their parents, but also in their breaking new ground. For instance, the children of hotel and motel owners have carried the achievements of their parents to new heights. By earning degrees in Hospitality Management from leading colleges and universities, they have professionalized their parents' occupations and gone from owning budget motels to acquiring luxury hotels. Other second-generation Indian Americans have chosen instead to diverge completely from their parents' occupations by becoming attorneys or entertainers, or by pursuing careers in sports and fashion.

Indian Americans have slowly begun to contribute to the areas of sports and entertainment. Although Indian Americans enjoy volleyball and basketball tournaments at community gatherings and favor tennis and golf for recreation, their innovation has been in developing a unique sports culture of cricket leagues. Cricket is a British legacy, and Indian Americans have popularized it by developing the sport in partnership with other Americans who share the same legacy (for example, Americans from Britain, Australia, Pakistan, Sri Lanka, and the West Indies.) Many local park districts have added the cricket "pitch"—the long runner strip in which the ball is bowled in cricket—to the baseball "diamond." Indian cricket lovers not only enjoy the game in their adopted land, but they hope it will catch on in the United States in the same way that soccer did when it was first imported from Europe.[49]

Indian-American student associations on college campuses nationwide have brought elements of Indian popular and folk culture within reach of Americans. By celebrating national Indian festivals such as Navratri and Diwali with folk dance routines in bhangra and *garba* and *dandia-ras*, and performing the classical dance styles of *Bharatanatyam* and *Kathak*, on the high-school and college stage, Indian-American youth have introduced a new generation of Americans to Indian culture while preserving it for themselves. The term *Bollywood* needs no introduction; most Americans recognize it as the name for the Indian movie industry based in Bombay (now called Mumbai). Cable TV channels are beaming Indian programs, while Bollywood movies, with English subtitles, regularly play at major multiplexes, catering to an ever-growing Indian-American population and adding yet another dimension to the globalization of entertainment.[50]

HELPING THEMSELVES, HELPING OTHERS

Indian-American women have achieved truly outstanding success in a variety of fields. With more than 50 percent in the workforce, they have stood shoulder to shoulder with men in their accomplishments. Women who worked behind the scenes, such as grandmothers who provided child care to enable their daughters and daughters-in-law to stay in the workforce, were as responsible for the community's achievements as the women who won top honors and recognition for their professional achievements. Women such as Indira Nooyi, President and Chief Financial Officer for Pepsico, Inc., and Lata Krishnan, cofounder of SMART Modular Technologies, Inc., are highly visible in the corporate world.

In the literary world, women writers such as Pulitzer Prize winner Jhumpa Lahiri, Chitra Banerjee Divakaruni, and

(continues on page 86)

ASTRONAUT KALPANA CHAWLA (1961–2003): A LEGACY OF INSPIRATION

"Even when I was in high school if people asked me what I wanted to do, I knew I wanted to be an aerospace engineer." With these words, Kalpana Chawla acknowledged that she was attracted to flying at an early age. As a teenager, she would watch small planes and gliders in the flying club in her hometown and dream of taking to the skies. She pursued an extraordinary career as the first Indian-American astronaut to fly into space.

Chawla's tragic death onboard the space shuttle *Columbia* on February 1, 2003, immortalized her in the annals of American history. She perished along with her crewmembers when the spacecraft blew up during reentry into Earth's atmosphere, 16 minutes before its scheduled landing. Chawla was posthumously awarded the Congressional Space Medal of Honor, the NASA Space Flight Medal, and the NASA Distinguished Service Medal. India renamed its weather satellite launched in 2002 Kalpana-1 in her memory.

Kalpana Chawla was born on July 1, 1961, in the small market town of Karnal, in northern India. She studied aeronautical engineering at Punjab Engineering College, came to the United States to acquire an M.S. from the University of Texas at Arlington (1984), and a Ph.D. from the University of Colorado (1988). She was selected by the National Aeronautical and Space Agency (NASA) in 1994, and after training, she received numerous assignments to work on technical issues. NASA said that her academic accomplishments, intense physical fitness, and experience as a pilot made her a natural choice.*

For Chawla, flying was not only a profession, but a passion. She was married to a flying instructor, Jean Pierre Harrison. She held commercial and instructor's licenses for a variety of aircraft and gliders, and enjoyed flying aerobatics and tail wheel planes. In 1997, she flew on STS-87 as a mission specialist and

Kalpana Chawla, one of seven crewmembers tragically killed in the Space Shuttle *Columbia* disaster on February 1, 2003, joined NASA in 1994 and served on her first mission in November 1997. The native of Karnal, India, immigrated to the United States in 1982 to pursue a Master of Science degree in aerospace engineering at the University of Texas at Arlington.

prime operator of the shuttle orbiter's robotic arm.

When asked in an interview where she finds her inspiration, she responded, "For me, definitely, it comes every day from people in all walks of life. It's easy for me to be motivated and inspired by seeing somebody who just goes all out to do something. For example, some of the teachers in high school. The amount of effort they put in to carry out their courses. The extra time they took to do experiments with us. . . . In general during my life, I would say I've been inspired by explorers—Shackleton, Lewis and Clark, Patty Wagstaff and Peter Matthiessen. . . . When I read about these people, I think the one thing that just stands out is their perseverance in how they carried out what they wished to carry out."

Chawla was awed by the grandeur of the universe. "We do science, we do experiments, but looking at Earth and appreciating the magnificence of it is easily the most touching thing you come back with," she said. Having made the ultimate sacrifice, Kalpana Chawla has herself become a source of awe and inspiration for an entire generation of young women.

---

* Daniel Lak, "South Asian News," *BBC Dispatches from Delhi* (November 20, 1997). Available online at *www.nasa.gov.*

(continued from page 83)

Canadian Bharati Mukherjee, wrote about the immigrant experience in ways that made their readers aware of the inner workings of the Indian-American mind. Indian-American women, too, formed organizations to support each other and nurture their identities as immigrant women. Among the earliest was the Club of Indian Women, formed in Chicago in 1978 to help isolated suburban women connect with one another. By 2005, a group of mostly second-generation women were active in building the Indus Women Leaders organization into a national forum to provide women with networking resources to help them achieve their life goals.

Social service organizations sprang up in the Indian-American community in the 1980s and 1990s, when new waves of immigrants with inadequate language and job skills began to enter the United States. Recognizing the need to help members of their own community, many dedicated visionaries founded organizations that have helped the poor, women, and the elderly. Such measures have helped to keep Indian Americans less dependent on welfare programs and have given the community a sense of achievement in addressing these problems.

Other activities, such as responding to crises in the homeland with generous outpourings of aid, have enabled Indian Americans to extend their volunteerism across national boundaries. When a devastating earthquake hit Gujarat in January 2001, a Gujarat Relief Fund was established to rebuild schools, community centers, and entire townships destroyed by the earthquake. Similarly, a tsunami relief fund raised hundreds of thousands of dollars in 2004 to aid victims of the disaster in India, Sri Lanka, and Indonesia.

What achievements are Indian Americans themselves most proud of? They are proud that they are one of the most affluent and well-educated groups in the United States. They are proud that they are giving back to their adopted country through their involvement and hard work. They are also proud that they give back to the motherland. Ultimately, through their connection to both India and the United States, they have redefined the meaning of immigration. No longer does it mean giving up the old land in order to adopt the new. They have managed to stay connected to both countries, and achieve their potential, thanks to the liberal atmosphere of the era in which they live and the willingness of both India and the United States to be closely connected in a world of globalization.

• Study Questions •

1. How have Indian Americans preserved their culture in the United States?

2. Do you think immigrant groups should be allowed to follow their own traditions? Why? Why not?

3. What role do religious institutions play in the lives of Indian Americans?

4. Why did Indian Americans form their own professional organizations? What purpose did these organizations have in connecting Indian Americans to their homeland?

5. What contributions have Indian Americans made to American popular culture, in arts, sports, and entertainment?

6. What kind of social services are needed in the Indian-American community? How do you think they compare with the needs of other immigrant groups?

7

Trouble in Utopia

Despite a general perception of affluence and record accomplishments for Indian Americans, they are faced with
many problems and challenges, mostly arising from their situation as immigrants. Oftentimes, they feel displaced and up-
rooted. They are looked upon with suspicion in their new home
by Americans who distrust foreigners. Even those who are born
and brought up in the United States are caught in the "perpet-
ual foreigner" syndrome, because of their skin color and facial
features.

The rapid growth of the Indian-American community
presented its own difficulties. As the community became
larger and more diversified, class divisions arose between rich
and poor immigrants, between established pioneers and still-
struggling newcomers. There was fragmentation along lines of
religion and language, and conflicts between the more tradi-
tion-minded and the more progressive-minded groups. The

Despite being looked upon with suspicion by Americans who distrust foreigners, many Indian Americans proudly support their adopted country. Pictured here are three Sikh men who are carrying American flags during a Fourth of July celebration in Philadelphia.

general prosperity of the community attracted the envy and prejudice of other Americans, who targeted Indian Americans for discrimination and violent hate crimes. Because of continued immigration and changes in the global arena—in America's

WHAT CHANGES?
WHAT STAYS THE SAME?

There are, indeed, sharp contrasts between the early Indian pioneers who came to the United States and those who came after 1965. As one second-wave immigrant put it, "The first Indian immigrants and the post-1965 Indian immigrants are two separate worlds. It is a class thing. They came from the farming, the lower class. We came from the educated middle class. We spoke English. We went to college. We were already assimilated in India before we came here."*

The early immigrants came mostly from one state of India (Punjab) and settled mostly in one state in the United States (California). They faced a hostile reception and struggled under discriminatory laws. The post-1965 immigrants, by contrast, came from many locales in India and settled throughout the United States. They were welcomed as professional elite, enjoyed the rights of citizenship, and were free to pursue their goals.

When the post-1965 Indian immigrants arrived in California, tensions arose between them and the older Punjabi immigrants. The newcomers disapproved of the Punjabi-Mexican marriages and the willingness of the earlier Punjabis to give up their beliefs and practices (such as shaving off their beards and discarding their turbans), in order to blend into American society. By contrast, the new Indians were proud of their religion and culture, which they were eager to pass on to their children.

Such tensions exist among many other immigrant communities, including Polish, Mexicans, and Chinese. The pioneers and the new Indian immigrants also share many commonalities, however, especially the experience of adapting to a new culture, putting down roots, and raising families—all the while trying to stay connected to the homeland of India.

---

* Quoted in Ronald Takaki, *Strangers from a Different Shore: A History of Asian Americans* (Boston: Little, Brown, 1989), 245.

relationships with India and other countries in the region, like Pakistan and Afghanistan—the challenges for Indian Americans are in a constant state of flux.

Immigrants who arrived in the United States in the 1960s and 1970s were pioneers who had to face their challenges without the aid of a welcoming or support group. They faced loneliness and yearning for the familiar environment of the homeland, and a sense of nostalgia that every immigrant experiences. As they became more used to their American life and started identifying with the new homeland, however, they faced yet another problem. Could they consider themselves truly American? How did Americans perceive them? How much of their homeland traditions should they cling to? How should they raise their children? Some developed strong identities as Indians within their homes but preferred to adopt a more American identity in the world outside. Those who visited India frequently were faced with the added challenge of being considered "foreigners" in their own homeland.

REDISCOVERING IDENTITY

The identity crisis was particularly acute for the younger generation. Many wanted desperately to be identified and accepted as American, but that was not easy, as demonstrated in the words of two young men who remembered their school days. From one:

> We got called names when we were kids—teepees, camel jockeys, Hindus. I got beat up plenty of times. I think guys got beat up more than girls. Once I walked home from high school. A car pulled up. Three seniors got out and proceeded to beat the life out of me. Right there on school property. Just because I was Indian.[51]

The pressures of having to get good grades in school and identify with Indian culture were overwhelming, as another young man pointed out:

It was so painful growing up here, and our parents were so busy going to work, they missed what we were going through, all that pain. Maybe in India getting straight As means you will be popular, but here you have to be doing other things, socially you feel so isolated. They didn't even understand we were going through that. My mother would say, "Today, you're going to Show and Tell, and you're going to talk about Diwali." I don't think she knew how embarrassing it was for me.[52]

The dilemma of mixed-race Indians in forming a cohesive identity is captured in the words of this American woman, who is still acutely conscious of her colonial heritage:

And after all, my Indian family is not so much a nice masala [mixture of powdered spices], however spicy one can be. We are not great keepers of tradition. We are a mess, a hodge-podge of not belonging; Muslims in India, Indians in Fiji, Muslim-Fiji-Indians in the United States (and this is just my father's side). Every disparate part of my family—Indian and Fijian on my father's side, Scottish and Native American on my mother's—originated in a land that has, at one point in the past, been colonized by the British. Such is the recent history of the world.[53]

The crisis of identity among young Indian Americans becomes even more problematic in cases where parents are rigidly traditional and refuse to understand the influences that their children bring from attending American schools and watching movies and television. Heated conversations about dating (generally frowned upon among Indian Americans), premarital sex (Indian Americans have stereotypes of Americans as permissive and promiscuous), and interracial marriages (opposed by those who are afraid of losing their culture) are the stuff of living-room debates. Caught between the desire to please their loving and protective parents, and the desire to be like their peers, Indian-American youth are truly between a rock and a hard place.

As the children grew into young adults in college, they sought their own solutions. Some became proud of their Indian heritage and learned more about it through college courses. Some created their own youth subcultures that revolved around fusion music clubs frequented by African-American and white youths.[54] Still others cracked under the pressure of trying to figure out where they belonged and went into deep depression or even committed suicide.

THE WORLD OF WOMEN

As immigrants in the United States, some women had the opportunity to acquire more education and pursue exciting careers, but others felt left out. One woman felt cheated and resentful of the sacrifices she had to make as a traditional Indian wife and mother:

> Your value system inside—you feel you have to take care of your husband. There is no money for us to go to college in America. Your husband has to establish himself first. My life got derailed from the day I got here. Whenever I try to get back on track, I find the rails are rusted.[55]

Not having extended family in the United States was difficult for the early arrivals because they were deprived of the support they could have had in raising their children and pursuing careers. Sometimes elderly parents from India were able to come to help alleviate the burden, but many others found balancing home and career a real challenge, especially with their traditional Indian husbands not sharing household responsibilities as equal partners. Consider this description of a motel-owning wife who did most of the work involved in running the motel but got little support from her husband:

> Women do most of the work involved in running motels.... Though she does hard work in the motel, she has no help in the kitchen or with other household work which is

traditionally considered "women's tasks." When asked if her husband ever helps her with the dishes, etc. Mrs. C's quick reply is, "No, never—I cannot think of him doing that!"[56]

Elderly Indian Americans also face problems as they confront their sunset years. Those who came to live with their children in the United States miss India. Some feel discarded and unappreciated as they outlive their usefulness as babysitters for their grandchildren. Many lack health insurance, access to good health care and transportation, and lead isolated and lonely lives. The Indian immigrants who came in the 1960s and 1970s are themselves aging and facing the prospect of living in retirement or nursing homes. It is a painful reality for them, because in India the practice of isolating the elderly in old-age homes is not well accepted. One widow who lives with her son and daughter-in-law confesses,

> I'm scared. In America, children always talk of moving out of the house. My daughter-in-law may also be feeling that all her American friends are living on their own while she has to live with a mother-in-law. Today, we may get along with our daughters-in-law. Tomorrow, we may not. My daughter-in-law lives in a different world in American society. Her friends may ask, "What! Your mother-in-law lives with you?" There is a saying that if you repeat a lie a thousand times it becomes the truth. What if the daughter-in-law also begins to believe that it is wrong to have your in-laws live with you?[57]

AN EASY TARGET

While Indian Americans were coping with evolving personal issues, the growth and diversity of the community presented new challenges. Large numbers of unskilled Indians were entering the country in the 1980s, when the economic recession made it hard for them to find good jobs. For comfort and security,

they started to cluster in ethnic enclaves. When their presence
became highly concentrated and visible, as in certain communities in New Jersey, they aroused the wrath of local residents,
who accused them of taking away their jobs. Gangs of white
youth, including a hate group calling itself "Dotbusters" (for
the dot or *bindi* that Indian women wear on their foreheads),
openly attacked Indian Americans, calling them racist names,
throwing stones, breaking into homes, and defacing their
houses of worship. In Hoboken, New Jersey, one Indian named
Navroze Mody was beaten to death by a gang of white and Hispanic youths on September 27, 1987. Scores of other attacks

In the wake of the terrorist attacks of September 11, 2001, Sikhs have
been persecuted due to the mistaken perception that they are Muslim
or Middle Eastern. Rajinder Singh Khalsa, who was brutally beaten
by five men outside a restaurant in the New York borough of Queens
in July 2004, is pictured here in front of a framed copy of the U.S.
Senate resolution that condemns hate crimes against Arab Americans,
Muslim Americans, South-Asian Americans, and Sikh Americans.

during this period brought to mind the racist violence directed toward Sikhs nearly a century ago.[58]

Indian Americans were targeted once again in the aftermath of the terrorist attacks of September 11, 2001, but this time, it was a case of mistaken identity. Because Sikh Americans, who wear turbans and grow their beards long, look similar to people from Afghanistan, they were attacked indiscriminately. There were two tragic cases in Arizona where Sikhs, mistaken for Afghans, were gunned down by white men. More than 600 ethnic-bias incidents against Americans perceived to be Muslim or Middle Eastern were reported in the media, and many of the victims were Indian American.[59]

INTERNAL TENSIONS

Within the community, there is a growing divide between the haves and have-nots. Though there is no overt class conflict, the rich are sometimes perceived as an elitist group, far removed from the concerns of the poor. The image of prosperity and lack of awareness of poverty issues has created a stereotype of a thriving community where everyone is imagined to be successful and without need of any public assistance. The result is that needy and deserving members of the group are denied social and financial assistance available to other groups, such as African Americans or Latinos, who are classified as underprivileged minorities.

Other lines of division within the community are related to language and religion. Indian Americans who are from one part of India may not socialize with Indian Americans who come from another part and speak another language. This is not because of any hostility or aversion of one group toward another but may be merely the result of a tendency to seek out the familiar and stay within a comfort zone. By the 1980s, there were enough Gujaratis, Punjabis, Tamils, Telugus, Bengalis, Malayalees, and other language groups in the United States to make such narrow identifications possible. One young woman complained about the restricted circle in which her parents lived: "My parents' friends are not even from South India, but Kannada, only Kannada. They're from Udipi, they've been all over India but . . . they have only Udipi friends. . . . I would like to see my parents have Indian friends who speak other languages."[60]

There are similar social divides between Indian Americans of different religious groups. Indian-American Muslims are more likely to fraternize with Muslims of other nationalities than with Indian-American Hindus. There has been no open hostility or interreligious conflict among these different groups of Indian Americans, however. Even when there have been religious disturbances and riots in India and other diaspora communities of Indians, Indian Americans have made conscious attempts to maintain harmony and act as a unified group.

In the 1990s, social service agencies arose in response to the needs of the underprivileged. These agencies offered English literacy classes, civics classes, free medical care, services for the elderly, and shelter for victims of domestic abuse. They also began to recognize the abuse and exploitation of a growing population of domestic workers and others in low-wage jobs. Workers' unions such as Awaaz and Andolan, and a taxi driver's union, sprang up in New York to protect their rights.

Other problems remained unaddressed. In many Indian-owned franchises in the newsstand and food service industries, workers were often taken advantage of by their own ethnic employers. Their problems went unacknowledged, because many of the immigrants were illegal and did not dare complain for fear of being discovered and deported. Problems of discrimination and unfair practices existed not only among low-wage workers but also among white-collar professionals who were paid lower wages, often denied promotions, and unable to achieve their full career potential.

After nearly 50 years of continuous growth, Indian Americans are worried that the tightening of immigration laws and increased visa restrictions will hurt the expansion of the community. There are still far more men than women (53 percent to 47 percent), and without a friendly immigration policy that allows family members to freely enter the United States, there is a danger of a greater imbalance. The presence of women is crucial for the growth of a stable community, as we saw from the negative experiences of the early Sikh immigrants. Other high-priority issues include the need to guard civil rights, eliminate hate crimes, and provide greater opportunities for the education and employment of the growing number of poor in the population. Most of all, the perception of Indian Americans, whether Hindu, Muslim, Sikh, or Christian, must be such that they are accepted as full Americans. Indians are trying to reach this goal, using all the tools available to them as citizens of a free democracy and especially by taking part in the democratic process, as we shall see in the next chapter.

• Study Questions •

1. How do you define identity? Why is it important?

2. How is Indian-American identity different for different individuals?

3. What is meant by "gender roles"? In what ways are problems faced by Indian immigrant women different from those faced by Indian immigrant men? How do they compare with problems faced by other American women?

4. Define a hate crime. Why do people commit such crimes? Why are Indian Americans targeted?

5. Is the diversity of a population a strength or a weakness? What impact does the diversity of the Indian-American population have on their lives?

8

Establishing a Political Voice

Unlike many other immigrant groups that came to the United States to flee poverty and oppression in their homeland, Indian Americans traditionally enjoyed political freedom and pride in their home country's democratic, secular traditions. Most of them were born after India had gained its independence, and they had developed strong nationalist feelings about their country. Having heard about America as the land of freedom and democracy, they expected to enjoy those same freedoms here in their pursuit of economic and social opportunities. Over the years, however, they learned that if they wanted to gain influence and shape their own lives, they would have to take an active part in the political process.

Indian Americans became politically involved well after they had achieved economic success. Indeed, because the vanguard group consisted of successful professionals and was generally embraced by mainstream America, they assumed there would be no need for a separate political identity. Most of them were unaware of the prejudicial treatment that Indians had been forced to tolerate in the immigration of the early 1900s. The economic success of these newer immigrants made them complacent and disinterested, and in the early years, they saw no reason to get involved in politics.

ASIAN INDIAN, SOUTH ASIAN, AND ASIAN AMERICAN

By 1980, however, a storm was brewing in the community about political identity. Should they continue to characterize themselves as "white" or "other" in the census forms, or should they seek "minority" status and risk being lumped with other historically underprivileged groups such as blacks and Hispanics? In an America that saw itself in terms of *white* and *black*, where did Indians fit in?

In a survey conducted in Chicago to explore these very questions, respondents answered that they saw themselves as neither white nor black, but *brown*. They demanded and secured a separate categorization as "Asian Indians" in the 1980 U.S. census. This was the birth of a new political identity for Indian Americans. Now, they could be quantified. They would know the socioeconomic assets and shortcomings of their own community and could begin to lay the building blocks of a political future. By the year 2000, however, their political clout still fell far short of their numeric strength and economic progress, though they had begun to make some small political gains.

The 1990s brought the evolution of a new identity for Indian Americans as "South Asian Americans," a group that included other brown people from Pakistan, Bangladesh, Sri Lanka, Nepal, and the Maldive Islands, countries of the Indian subcontinent that share the cultural heritage of Indian Americans. A host of organizations came under the South Asian banner, such as South Asian Students' Associations (SASA) on university campuses nationwide, the South Asian Journalists' Association,

South Asian American Leaders of Tomorrow, and the South Asian American Policy and Research Institute.

As South Asians, Indian Americans were also encouraged to identify with the larger Asian-American population. Asian-American history and activism go back to the 1960s era of civil rights struggles, and even further back to the early Asian immigration of the nineteenth century. Their longer experience and greater numbers could help Indian Americans secure a place at the political table. In schools and colleges, studies of the Indian American experience fall under the umbrella of Asian-American studies. Despite the obvious advantages of coalition building, Indian Americans are still held back from working closely with other Asian Americans by their cultural differences and narrower interests.

LEARNING THE ROPES IN POLITICS

It is said that a community becomes politically organized only when it feels threatened, when there are enough poor and marginalized people in it to mobilize for action. That time came for Indian Americans in the 1980s, when their numbers grew significantly and they were faced with a host of problems such as job discrimination, racial attacks, and restrictive immigration laws.

The Indo-American Democratic Organization (IADO) is one of the first political organizations to be formed with the explicit goal of encouraging Indian Americans to participate in the political process. Founded in 1980 by four Indian activists, the organization struggled in the early years to get Indians involved. "Indians are only keen on cultural extravaganzas, they are not interested in issue-oriented politics," said Ranjit Ganguly, one of its founding members. "In fact, to most Indians here, politics is a dirty word. They don't realize that if you don't organize politically, you don't exist, at least in the eyes of the government."[61]

IADO began to conduct voter registration drives and educate the public on the positions of different political candidates on various issues, so they would know how to vote in their own best interest. IADO members went as delegates to the Democratic National conventions, and worked closely with legislators such as Congresswoman Jan Schakowsky, whose Ninth Congressional District in Illinois includes a large Indian-American community on Chicago's northside. They worked on issues

Among the most prominent Indian Americans involved in the political arena is U.S. Representative Bobby Jindal. The Louisiana native was elected to Congress in November 2004 and is pictured here with his wife, Supriya, and his daughter, Selia Elizabeth, after earning the Republican nomination for governor in October 2003.

such as redistricting, where boundaries of political districts are redrawn after every census to accommodate population shifts.

Wealthy Indian Americans made hefty individual contributions to both Democrats and Republicans. For instance, in 2004, the cochairman of finance for President George W. Bush's campaign in Florida was an Indian-American cardiologist who raised $20 million.[62] This type of activity helped individuals develop personal relationships with politicians, but it did not necessarily help the community. As the community began to mature politically, there was a call to marshal these individual contributions and, cutting across party lines, channel them for the greater good of Indian Americans.

Whereas urban Indian Americans tended to identify largely with Democrats, more and more Indians in the suburbs joined the Republican Party. In 2004, they helped elect Republican Congressman Bobby Jindal to office in Louisiana. Indeed, when it comes to electing one of their own ethnicity, Indian Americans, both Democrats and Republicans, might support a candidate no matter which political party he or she belongs to. In 1994, the Indian American Center for Political Awareness (IACPA) was founded in New York with the objective of reaching out to all Indian Americans, regardless of party affiliation, and lobbying on their behalf on issues of immigration and voting rights, and fighting hate crimes and defamation.

GETTING OUT THE VOTE

One of the basic requirements of political involvement is citizenship. Naturalization, the process by which an immigrant becomes a citizen, was the goal of many immigrants, and as soon as they became eligible, usually after five years of residency in the United States, they applied for citizenship. Many wanted to become citizens so they would be allowed to sponsor their relatives and speed up the process of immigration. In 2000, about three-fourths of Indian Americans were foreign-born, and of these, about 40 percent, or 4 out of 10, had become naturalized citizens. This is the same rate at which other for-eign-born groups also become citizens. Other advantages of citizenship are the right to many social welfare programs for the poor and the elderly, and the right to vote.

The voting rate among Indian-American citizens, however, is lower than the national average. Only 57 percent of eligible Indian Americans are registered voters (compared to 67 per-cent of the general population), and only 38 percent voted in the 2000 presidential elections, compared to 46 percent of the general population. Political activists like Gopal Raju, founder of IACPA, urge greater voter turnout: "One major reason why the Indian American community lacks political clout is because of our lack of voter turnout. . . . Campaign contributions can only do so much. We need to demonstrate we have the votes to back our issues up."[63]

Indian Americans do not constitute "voting blocs" in the same way that some other groups, such as African Americans and Latinos, do. (When entire districts are occupied by people of a certain ethnicity, or when they all tend to vote the same way on a particular issue, they form a "voting bloc.") Though there are small pockets of concentration of Indian Americans in certain parts of the cities and suburbs, generally speaking, they are still too scattered and small in number to form powerful voting blocs.

In some states, where concentrations of Indian voters are high enough, these blocs have managed to get Indian Ameri-cans elected to public office. For instance, in 2001, Democrat Upendra Chivukula was elected to the State Assembly in New Jersey, a state with a heavy population of Indian Americans. Other Indian Americans, however, like State Senator Satveer Choudhary of Minnesota and House Delegate Kumar P. Barve of Maryland, have attained political office by appealing to the larger mainstream population.

Women have also made some inroads into political activ-ism and achieving elected office. Swati Dandekar is an Iowa

State Assembly representative (elected in 2002 and 2004) whose achievements are all the more remarkable because she was born and educated in India and gained her local community support through her volunteerism. In 2001, Rena Van Tine was appointed as an associate judge in Cook County, Illinois, and is the first female Indian-American judge in the United States. Other notable female Indian-American activists include Ann (Lata) Kalayil, first female president of IADO and Super Delegate to the 2000 National Democratic Convention.

On the whole, Indian Americans have not taken a firm, unified stand in politics. Their economic success has not translated

State Representative Swati Dandekar listens to a floor debate during a special session of the Iowa Legislature in September 2004. Although she has lived in Marion, Iowa, for more than three decades, Dandekar did not emigrate from India until she was 22.

directly into political success, and they need to work together more cohesively as a community on national issues of importance to them. There has been a political awakening, however, and it is likely that in the future, when faced with important challenges, they will work together. There is also an expectation that second- and third-generation Indian Americans will become more active in the political process.

INDO-CANADIAN POLITICS

Canada has an official policy of multiculturalism (unlike the United States), with a legal framework and a minister of state for multiculturalism. The government's plan of action is to rid the country of racism and bring together people of all ethnic, racial, and religious backgrounds. There are many laws, policies, activities, and programs to combat hate crimes, but racism remains a serious problem, with 33 percent of South Asian men (one in three) reporting that they felt discriminated against.[64] Still, Indo-Canadians have made their mark in politics much more effectively than Indian Americans, with several elected representatives in the British Columbia, Ontario, and Alberta legislatures. There are currently eight Indo-Canadian members of Parliament: Herb Dhaliwal, Gurbax Singh Malhi, Navdeep Singh Bains, Rahim Jaffer, the husband-wife team of Gurmant and Nina Grewal, Keith Martin, and Deepak Oberoi. Another prominent Indo-Canadian involved in politics is Ujjal Dosanjh, who served as premier of British Columbia before being elected as a member of the Canadian Parliament and being appointed health minister in 2004.[65]

HOMELAND POLITICS

Indians in North America have also taken keen interest in the politics of the homeland. Whenever prominent political figures from India visit North America, Indian Americans rally together to welcome them. The major Indian political parties, such as the BJP (Bharatiya Janata Party) and the Indian National Congress, have alliances and support groups in the United States—

for example, Overseas Friends of the BJP and Overseas Friends of Indian Congress. By working hand in hand with Indian politicians and other Indians of the oikumene, Indian Americans were instrumental in getting the Indian government to grant them dual citizenship in 2004.

Indian Americans also lobbied for better India–U.S. relations and helped form the India Caucus, a body of legislators from both major political parties in Washington dedicated to advancing the interests of India in the United States. Thanks partly to the efforts of Indian Americans and the politicians they supported, there was a marked improvement in relations between India and the United States in the 1990s. In 1999, when India became a nuclear nation, many Indian Americans found themselves defending India's action and justifying it. Their efforts to bring the two nations together culminated in the visit of President Bill Clinton to India in 2000. In subsequent years, Indian Americans found themselves caught up in other international issues, such as the debate on outsourcing.[66]

THE ACTIVIST AGENDA

The same developments in the community that galvanized Indian Americans into political involvement also turned them into activists. The younger generation of Indian Americans became painfully aware of their minority status in the United States for the first time during the anti-Indian violence in New Jersey. Activist groups such as South Asian Alliance for Action (SAAFA) and South Asian American Leaders of Tomorrow (SAALT) were formed to educate the public and advocate for vigorous prosecution of hate crimes. SAALT organizes activities on October 2, the birthday of Mahatma Gandhi, as a day of community service, both to honor the great leader and to encourage activism and volunteerism.[67]

Other issues that came to the fore in the late 1980s involved abuses within the Indian-American community. There was a high incidence of domestic violence, abandonment, child abuse and neglect, and sexual and criminal assault. The more conservative Indian Americans, anxious to keep up the model minority myth refused to acknowledge that such problems existed. Indian-American women activists nevertheless took the initiative to establish shelters for victims of domestic abuse, and soon several of them sprang up throughout the nation, revealing the seriousness of the problem.[68] These social service agencies addressed the special needs of South Asian women and children arising from their cultural differences in language, dress, food, religion, family structures, and values. Often, women and children were suffering violence and abuse rather than seeking help from friends and family because of the stigma attached to divorce, and these domestic abuse shelters were their last resort.

Other social service agencies sprang up to teach new immigrants how to read and write English and adjust to American society. They conducted civics classes, so Indians could learn enough about American history and government to pass the citizenship exam. They provided free medical care for those without health insurance and educated seniors about public benefits available to them. One such agency, called the Indo-American Center, in Chicago, also welcomes school and college students to learn more Indian-American history by interacting with the immigrants themselves.[69]

Indian-American activists are also championing causes in the wider community. The North American South Asian Bar Association (NASABA) estimates there are 5,000 lawyers of South Asian origin in the United States and Canada who are engaged in fighting crime, overturning wrongful convictions, and protecting the rights of the innocent. Famous names include Georgetown University Law Professor Neal Katyal, who criticized President George W. Bush's detention policies, and Kamala Harris (daughter of an Indian mother and African-American father), who was elected district attorney in San Francisco in 2003, the first woman of color to hold that post in California.[70] Urvashi Vaid, a law-school graduate and American Civil Liberties

Union (ACLU) staff member, served on the Board of Directors of the National Gay and Lesbian Institute and became executive director of its Policy Institute.[71]

When South Asian taxi drivers employed in New York felt the burden of unfair laws in 1996, they formed a labor union under the leadership of an Indian American, Bhairavi Desai.

MODEL MINORITY MYTH

Why should Indian Americans worry when America calls them "a model minority"? Isn't that a label to be proud of? Imagine being held up as a shining example to others, especially other immigrants and ethnic groups who are still struggling to find their way. Every time a politician wants to get the approval of the Indian-American community, he or she is likely to praise the "family values" and the "work ethic" that has enabled Indian Americans to succeed. Pointing to income and education statistics (which lump not only all Indian Americans but all Asian Americans, as a group, into one category), many people contend that Indian Americans do not experience any racial discrimination and have no need of public assistance.

The "model minority" stereotype emerged in the 1960s, when the media suggested that Japanese and Chinese were self-sufficient and able to succeed because of family support. At the time, the question was raised, "Why should the government spend billions of dollars to uplift other ethnic groups when Asian Americans were able to move ahead on their own?" Asians were held up as a model group that other minorities should strive to follow.* Likewise, Indian Americans themselves are not always aware of the dangers of this label. Any label that is imposed on immigrants by the host or dominant society should be examined carefully.

---

* Vijay Prashad, "Crafting Solidarities," in Lavina Dhingra Shankar and Rajini Srikanth, eds., *A Part, Yet Apart* (Philadelphia, Pa.: Temple University Press, 1998), 109.

Vijay Bali (center, blue shirt) and several members of New York City's Yellow Cab Drivers Association protest the city's plan to require cab drivers to carry more insurance. Indian Americans such as Bali and Bhairavi Desai, who formed the New York Taxi Workers Alliance (NYTWA), have worked to create better living and working conditions for their members.

The New York Taxi Workers Alliance (NYTWA) represents 6,000 taxi drivers from more than 90 countries. The group staged historic strikes in 1998 and 2004 to help secure better living and working conditions for many ethnic groups, including Black Africans.[72] Desai, Executive Director and cofounder of NYTWA, is a winner of the Ford Foundation's 2005 Leadership for Change award and has been described as having "a gentle, girl-next-door look" but also capable of being "the toughest person across the negotiating table or picket lines." As one of the first Indian Americans to commit herself full time to an empowerment, nonprofit organization, she serves as a role model for other Indian American activists.[73]

Indian-American activists work to bring about social and economic change in India, as well. The American India

Foundation connects communities and resources across the United States and India, by providing skilled American workers to India in a program called the Service Corps. It donates computers and software and training to underprivileged schools and helps Indian craftspeople build their skills and sell their products. The India Development Society in Chicago raises funds to help villages in India create and maintain their own self-sustaining development projects. ASHA for Education supports the cause of elementary education in the poorest regions of India, whereas Indicorps, founded in 2001 by siblings Anand, Roopal, and Sonal Shah, helps young Indian Americans reconnect with their heritage by providing them with the opportunity to do community work in India at the grassroots level.

• Study Questions •

1. Why do Indian Americans need to be politically organized? Identify some ways in which Indian Americans are organizing themselves politically.

2. What is naturalization? What are the advantages of becoming naturalized?

3. What political successes have Indian Americans achieved?

4. Do you think immigrants should be involved in homeland politics? Why? Why not? Can you think of other immigrant groups who are involved in the politics of their homeland?

5. Who are "activists"? Why are they important to society?

6. Identify three areas in which Indian-American activists have helped Indian Americans as well as other Americans. How have they done this?

9

Famous Indian Americans

or some immigrants, the very act of moving from the comfortable confines of their homeland to the uncharted territories of another country forces them to think in new ways,
challenging them and pushing them to heights of creativity and
accomplishment. Their efforts have led to personal and professional achievements that have brought them honors and recognition, whereas others have worked quietly behind the scenes to
make a difference.

Any attempt to capture the full range of interesting and exciting things that Indian Americans have accomplished will fall
far short of identifying all the deserving and outstanding individuals. It can, however, bring to light the special characteristics
of Indian-American contributions to the building of America.
Here, then, is a Hall of Fame of Indian Americans—not a complete list by any means but hopefully a satisfying sample. Our
list of notables runs the gamut of "movers and shakers" in a

wide variety of fields, from science and technology, business, academia, arts and letters, movies, sports, and politics.

THE WHIZ KIDS OF SILICON VALLEY

Because India has the second-largest pool of engineers and scientists in the world, it is not surprising that some of the biggest names in the computer and software development industry are

Vinod Khosla, the cofounder of Sun Microsystems, speaks at the Asia Society's 25th Annual Dinner Gala in May 2005. Khosla was one of five honorees who were presented with the Outstanding Asian American Entrepreneur Award at the event in New York.

Indian Americans. *Forbes* and *Fortune* magazines have listed the following Indian Americans among the richest and most successful American entrepreneurs: Vinod Dham, acclaimed "Father of the Intel Pentium Processor"; Sabeer Bhatia, founder of Hotmail; Vinod Khosla, cofounder of Sun Microsystems; Naveen Jain, founder and president of InfoSpace.com; Kanwal Rekhi, whom *Forbes* called "sage to Silicon Valley's affluent Indian community"; and Sanjiv Sidhu, cofounder and CEO of i2 Technologies.

Other notables include Gururaj Deshpande, head of Sycamore Networks, who graduated with a Ph.D. in data communications from Queens University in Kingston, Canada, and is widely respected for his contributions to education, particu-

THE LANGUAGE OF TECHNOLOGY

Among the hi-tech stars in the Indian-American firmament, each one of whom deserves a detailed account, the story of Sabeer Bhatia stands out as both unique and typical of Silicon Valley success. This pioneer in the field of Web-based e-mail cofounded Hotmail Corporation in 1996 and guided it through rapid growth, until it was bought by Microsoft Corporation in 1998.

In a 2001 interview, Bhatia confessed that when he first landed in the United States with $250 in his pocket and butterflies in his stomach, "I felt I had made a big mistake. I knew nobody. People looked different, it was hard for them to understand my accent and me to understand theirs. I felt pretty lonely." When pursuing his Master of Science degree at Stanford University, however, he was inspired by such Silicon Valley celebrities as Steve Jobs of Apple Computers and Vinod Khosla, who cofounded Sun Microsystems, and "realized they were human. And if they could do it, I could do it, too."

Working as a hardware engineer at Apple after graduation, he created Javasoft, a way of using the Web to create a personal

larly MIT's Deshpande Center for Technological Innovation. The crash of the stock market and the dot.com bust in 2000 hit Indian Americans very hard, but their faith in the long-term prospects of computer technology remains unshaken and they continue to dominate this industry.

BRANCHING OUT WITH SCIENCE AND TECHNOLOGY

Indian Americans carry their technological expertise into a wide variety of fields, including academia, business, and the social sphere. In Illinois, leading Indian-American academics—professors Bala Balachandran and Deepak Jain, Dean of Northwestern University's Kellogg School of Management—founded and help

database where users could keep schedules, to-do lists, and other personal information. He and his Apple colleague Jack Smith came up with the idea of adding e-mail to Javasoft, making it possible to access it from any computer, anywhere on the planet. It was a simple and revolutionary idea. They picked the name Hotmail, which included the letters "html"—the programming language used to write Web pages.

Finding investors to help him develop this idea was a difficult task. He knocked on many doors and was refused many times before he found venture capitalists who put up the money he needed. In 1998, he sold his company to Microsoft for $400 million. In 2002, with more than a quarter of a million subscribers signing up worldwide, the company was the world's largest e-mail provider, worth $6 billion.*

* Stuart Whitmore, "Driving Ambition: How a Bangalore Whizkid Became a Silicon Valley Posterboy," *Asiaweek.com*, 2001. Available online at *www.asiaweek.com/asiaweek/technology/990625/bhatia.html.*

run a program that conducts annual seminars on doing business in India. Rajat Gupta, a graduate of the Harvard Business School, is the first India-born CEO of a billion-dollar transnational company, McKinsey and Company. Satyen "Sam" Pitroda is credited with having created a communication network that provides the most remote rural areas in India with telephone kiosks run by independent small businesspeople.

Indian-American women have also excelled in technology. After graduating from India's top colleges, they have often continued their education in the United States, before gaining access to the boardroom. Padmasree Warrior is executive vice president and chief technology officer for Motorola and leads a global team of 4,600 technologists. Arati Prabhakar served as the director of the U.S. National Institute of Standards and Technology (1993–1997) and manages a billion-dollar fund that invests in the electronic industry.[74]

Thousands of Indian Americans have contributed their talents and expertise to the growth of America's premier institutions, such as NASA, Fermilab, and Argonne National Laboratories. Indian Americans have also worked in university settings to make scientific breakthroughs. The Nobel Laureate Dr. Hargobind Khurana was professor of biology and chemistry at the Massachusetts Institute of Technology when he won the Nobel Prize for physiology or medicine in 1968. He laid the foundation of modern genetic engineering by creating a biologically active synthetic gene. He helped start the process of mapping the human genome.[75]

Another Nobel Laureate, Dr. S. Chandrasekhar (1910–1995) is described as the "greatest mathematical astrophysicist of our generation." Dr. Chandrasekhar was awarded the Nobel Prize in physics in 1983 for his work on the nature of stars and black holes. His equations explained the underlying physics behind the creation of white dwarfs, neutron stars, and other compact objects. He wrote many books on stellar structure and evolution, and relativistic astrophysics, including *Newton's Principia for the Common Reader.* The world's most powerful X-ray tele-scope launched by NASA is named the Chandra X-Ray Obser-vatory, in his honor.[76]

In the field of medicine, the collective contribution of Indian-American doctors and health-care workers is well known, but Indian Americans have ventured into other branches of healing, as well. For example, spiritual healing through an alternative form of Indian healing called *Ayurveda* has been popularized by world-renowned endocrinologist Dr. Deepak Chopra. Dr. Abraham Verghese, a distinguished writer and physician, wrote a powerful book on AIDS in small-town Mississippi called *My Own Country: A Doctor's Story.* A fine ex-ample of Indian-American doctors' commitment to the home-land is Dr. Dharmapuri Vidyasagar, director and founder of the department of neonatology at the University of Illinois at Chi-cago Hospitals, who has carried his expertise to India and has done extensive work among the rural population.

AN EXPLOSION OF CREATIVE WRITING

In the field of arts and letters, Indians in North America have made a stunning impact and gained a wide readership with their literary accomplishments. Whether born in India or elsewhere, these writers have a wealth of experience in traveling and living in other countries and write with great sensitivity about India and the immigrant experience.

A. K. Ramanujam (1929–1993), poet, translator, linguist, and folklorist, taught at the University of Chicago and trans-lated poems and folktales from his native Kannada and Tamil into English. In 1983, he received a MacArthur Foundation Fel-lowship and the title of *Padmashri* from the Government of In-dia for his contributions to Indian literature and linguistics.[77] Ved Mehta, totally blind from the age of four, has produced an impressive body of fiction, nonfiction, and journalistic works, the most voluminous among them being the autobiographical *Continents of Exile.* Amitav Ghosh is another widely known and respected Indian writer who has won numerous awards for his travelogues, political essays, and science fiction.

The work of Chitra Banerjee Divakaruni, author and poet, has been published in more than 50 magazines and included in more than 30 anthologies. Her first book of short stories, *Arranged Marriage*, has won critical acclaim and many awards. Jhumpa Lahiri, who writes poignantly of the nostalgia and yearning of ordinary immigrants and their everyday lives, won the Pulitzer Prize for fiction in 2000 with her collection of short stories *Interpreter of Maladies*.

There are many Indian Americans in the field of journalism, who either write for newspapers or magazines, or work in broadcasting. Among the more well known are Fareed Zakaria, editor of *Newsweek International*, and Sanjay Gupta, CNN medical correspondent. The founder of SAJA (South Asian American Journalists Association) is Sreenath Srinivasan, a Columbia University journalism professor and a technology reporter for television.[78] The husband-and-wife team of Sonny Mehta (editor in chief of the publishing house Alfred A. Knopf) and Gita Mehta (who has written extensively on the Western perception of Indian culture and history in works like *Karma Cola: Marketing the Mystic East*) are well known in American literary circles.

Bharati Mukherjee is a writer whose life and works straddle India, Canada, and the United States. Her novels reflect her own struggle with identity as an exile from India and expatriate in Canada finally coming to terms with her immigrant status in the United States. She is best known for *The Middleman and Other Stories*, which won the National Book Critics Circle Award for Best Fiction in 1988.[79] Rohinton Mistry is another famous Indo-Canadian writer whose novels about family and community amid the grinding poverty of his native India have earned comparisons with Charles Dickens. His novel *A Fine Balance* was a selection for talk-show host Oprah Winfrey's Book Club in 2001.[80]

Author Jhumpa Lahiri is pictured here shortly after she was named the 2000 Pulitzer Prize winner in fiction for her book of short stories *Interpreter of Maladies*. The best seller has been translated into 29 languages and also earned the PEN/Hemingway Award and *The New Yorker* Debut of the Year award.

THE WORLD OF ENTERTAINMENT

The creative talents and special gifts of Indian Americans have blossomed in fields not traditionally associated with them, such as moviemaking, sports, and popular entertainment. Some individuals have sprung to the limelight through the force of their creative energies and ability to capture the imagination of American audiences. Others have created popular subcultures that have grabbed the attention of music or theater lovers. Bands like *Funkadesi*, cultural events such as *Artwallah*, and theater groups such as *Rasaka* give Indian Americans the opportunity to work as DJs, musicians, and actors, occupations they cherish even while they hold down "day jobs" as attorneys, computer engineers, or physicians. There are locally produced radio and TV shows featuring Western and Indian programs in almost every major U.S. city with a large South Asian population.

Hollywood has attracted a host of aspiring second-generation Indian Americans, many of whom are struggling for recognition, although others have already made their mark. Some are making a living by playing small roles in drama series and television sitcoms, and others, like Ajay Naidu (whose credits include *Office Space*), have achieved modest success. One Indian-American actor, Kal Penn, who has starred in acclaimed films such as *American Desi,* also has a mainstream hit to his credit, *Harold and Kumar Go to White Castle.* A new TV sitcom, *Never Mind Nirvana,* about an Indian-American family brings the Indian-American culture straight into America's living rooms.

Among the luminaries in the film world are M. Night Shyamalan and Deepa Mehta. M. Night Shyamalan is an Indian-American director who achieved great success with his 1999 blockbuster *The Sixth Sense,* a supernatural thriller about a young boy who sees dead people. The movie includes a much-talked about surprise ending, which turned it into a huge moneymaker that also proved to be a critical favorite. It earned six Academy Award nominations, including Best Director and

Best Picture. Other Hollywood movies Shyamalan is famous for include *Unbreakable, Signs,* and *The Village.* He also earned kudos as the screenwriter for the smart, funny script of *Stuart Little.* The Indo-Canadian filmmaker Deepa Mehta is known

Among the most prominent Indian-American filmmakers is M. Night Shyamalan. A native of Madraf, India, Shyamalan has garnered praise for many of his movies, including *The Sixth Sense*, which was nominated for six Academy Awards.

for her trilogy named after the elements *Earth*, *Fire*, and *Water*, all movies dealing with cultural taboos and political tensions in India. Her greatest commercial success, however, came with her light-hearted romantic comedy *Hollywood/Bollywood*.

SPORTS ICONS

The world's number-one golf player in 2005 was Vijay Singh, a Fiji-Indian-American who has run neck and neck with Tiger Woods for supremacy on the PGA (Professional Golfers' Association) tour. Winner of the 2000 Masters and 1998 and 2004 PGA Championships, he has won millions of dollars and earned a reputation as a hard-working, hard-hitting player.[81]

Indian Americans are extremely proud of Mohini Bharadwaj, U.S. Olympic Gymnast and 2004 silver medalist in the women's team competition. A graduate of the University of California at Los Angeles, she has won numerous world championships in floor exercise, vault, and uneven bars thanks in large part to her competitive spirit. As she puts it, "The reason I do gymnastics is I love to compete. I love the adrenaline, the pressure, the satisfaction of doing well."[82]

Among Indo-Canadians, Emanuel Sandhu is one of the top male figure skaters in the world. He scored a stunning victory over the reigning world champion in 2003 at the Grand Prix Finals in Colorado Springs, Colorado. Other notables include Manny Malhotra, the first player of Indian descent to play in the National Hockey League with the Columbus Blue Jackets, and Ajay Baines, who played ice hockey for the NHL's Chicago Black Hawks and the American Hockey League's Norfolk Admirals.

REPRESENTING THE PEOPLE

In politics, there are two names that stand out because of their achievements at the national level—the aforementioned U.S. Congressman Bobby Jindal and Canadian Minister of Health Ujjal Dosanjh.

Jindal (Republican), a native of Louisiana and a Rhodes scholar, first rose to prominence when he ran for governor of Louisiana in 2003. Though he lost the race, he became widely known and highly respected for his role in strengthening and improving the Medicare program in Louisiana, and as senior health policy advisor to President George W. Bush. When he ran for Congress in 2004, the Indian-American community gave him strong support, regardless of their individual party affiliation, so proud were they to have one of their own elected to national office.

Ujjal Dosanjh (New Democrat Party), who was born in Dosanjh Kalan, near Phagwara, in India, came to Canada via England. He was a millworker and a teacher at a community college before he established his own law practice in Vancouver. Active in the human rights and social justice arena, he was elected to office and held many provincial cabinet positions before becoming the thirty-third premier of British Columbia in 2000. Recognition at the federal level came in 2004, when he was elected Member of Parliament from Vancouver South and appointed Minister of Health.

For every Indian American who has achieved fame and fortune, there are thousands of others who are making a difference in the lives of the people they touch, but whose names remain unknown beyond their immediate circle. There are artists, priests, cooks, social workers, grandparents, behind-the-scenes workers in shops and restaurants, many of whom cannot speak English and live largely within their own ethnic world. They are heroes to the people whose lives they may have transformed or influenced deeply. It is a matter of great pride for Indian Americans that so many in their midst are making such significant contributions to the building of America, but it is even more satisfying when they are recognized by the wider society, so they can serve as role models for everyone.

• Study Questions •

1. How do you explain the extraordinary success of Indian Americans in the field of computer technology?

2. How are the achievements of first-generation or immigrant parents different from those of their second-generation children?

3. Do you think Indians are well represented in the media? Why? Why not? How do they compare with other Asian groups? Other immigrant groups?

4. How do you define "success"? Do you think immigrant groups have different definitions of success than the wider American society?

5. Do you know of other successful Indian Americans? How did they become successful?

10

Connecting
the Dots

Remember Moola Singh, who left his wife behind in Punjab in 1911? Or Chandra Lachman Singh and his wife Nerissa, who came from Grenada and lived in Chicago until 1989? Or Vijay Singh, millionaire golfer, the Fiji-American of Indian ancestry? How do we connect the disparate stories of these Americans? How well does the "Indian-American" label serve to describe these immigrants? How were their individual fortunes affected by the times and places in which they lived? What about a person like California congressman Dalip Singh Saund, who broke the mold and rose to unimaginable heights despite the prejudice of the times?

There is yet another Singh story, very different from these. Singh Development Company, a well-known name in the residential and commercial building industry in Michigan, owes its origins to a Sikh Indian immigrant who left his village in India in 1921, headed for California, and came to Detroit, before bringing over his grandsons, who founded a successful construction business. This third-generation, family-owned and -operated concern stands out as a rare example of continuous living history. Gurmale Grewal, CEO of the company and grandson of the original immigrant, Sarwan S. Grewal, attributes his success to the work ethic of his close-knit family and adherence to their Sikh values and roots, reinforced every year by family trips to India.[83]

When we put together the stories of individual Indian Americans and create the history of a group, we see how both their personal lives and their collective histories are fraught with ups and downs. The early Punjabi farmers, along with other Asians, struggled against injustice, but they devised their own strategies for survival, intermarrying with Mexicans and working the system in ways that suited them. As their numbers dwindled, however, their identity as Indian Americans became obscured. New immigration after 1965 brought renewed interest in their history, so that their legacy of struggle and resilience remains an inspiration, not only to other Indian Americans but all immigrant groups.

NEW AND OLD AND IN BETWEEN

The "new" Indian Americans, so different from the old and yet with so many common traits, are becoming increasingly diverse. They are coining new terms to describe themselves, using words like *Desi,* which, loosely translated, means "of your own country." The word encompasses other people from the subcontinent, like the Pakistanis and Bangladeshis, who share their culture. As "South Asians," they are coming together under a politically useful identity that enables them to rise above regional differences.

From thinking about how other Americans view them, Indian Americans are now able to see themselves in new ways, even laugh at themselves, using acronyms such as ABCDs (American Born Confused Desis, to describe second-generation Indian

Americans caught between many cultures), FOBs (Fresh Off the Boats, to describe their greenhorn, newly arriving compatriots), and NRIs (officially stands for Nonresident Indians, but increasingly joked about as Nonreturning Indians, who nurture a myth of retirement in the homeland but will never act it out). They are gaining new confidence and new visibility, and continuing to make their mark everywhere, from neighborhood marketplaces to the boardrooms of Wall Street.

In charting the course taken by Indian Americans in the building of the United States, we can see how their contributions in the 1960s and 1970s were mainly in the field of science, engineering, and medicine. Soon afterward, they ventured into other areas, as small retailers, hoteliers, and restaurateurs, and over the years became big names in the multinational corporate world, maturing as businesspeople and entrepreneurs. In the 1990s, they helped in the development of the American technological era through their drive and innovation. American businesses, local and state governments, and other employers are recognizing the value of having a diverse workforce and recruiting Indians in larger numbers than ever before, fueling new immigration.

Young Indian Americans are setting the pace in many of the traditional fields chosen by their parents, but they are also breaking new ground. Take the Broadway show *Bombay Dreams*, which had a successful run in New York after playing to packed audiences in London. The real story behind "Bombay Dreams" is not just that it brought a Bollywood-style musical to mainstream American audiences, but that it enabled second-generation Indian Americans like Manu Narayanan and Anisha Nagarajan, both of whom grew up in Pittsburgh, to realize their own dreams by starring in a production about their homeland. It also enabled them to venture into a world unexplored by their parents' generation.[84] As Indian Americans vigorously pursue their own individual ambitions in the United States, they are transforming the way Americans eat, work, play, and live.

PERMEATING AMERICAN CULTURE AND SOCIETY

Indian-American influence can now be seen in many different aspects of American culture. Indian staples such as *saag paneer* (a spinach and cheese dish), chicken *tikka masala* (a spicy curried dish), and *naan* (a fluffy bread) are stocked regularly on supermarket shelves side by side with pizzas and tacos. No need to search out a "mom and pop" grocery store if you want Indian eggplant or bitter gourd or curry leaves—you'll find them where you shop. Bollywood blockbusters like *Lagaan: Once Upon a Time in India*, *Monsoon Wedding*, and *Bend It Like Beckham* are available for rent at Blockbuster video stores. Many Americans now know that in addition to Christmas, Hanukkah, Kwanzaa, and Eid Al-Fitr, there is a holiday called Diwali that is celebrated in neighborhoods, temples, and even in the White House.[85] Not by their presence alone, but through their activism, Indian Americans are demanding attention. Witness the electronic petition to the U.S. Postal Service, signed by more than 250,000 people, to issue a postage stamp to commemorate Diwali.

When faced with adversity, such as hate crimes or racial discrimination, both in the workplace and in society, Indian Americans have fought back through organized effort and by raising their individual voices. According to the New York City Commission on Human Rights, South Asians in New York are living with racial discrimination every day, and the wrongful detention of people based on the color of their skin or their religion continues in the atmosphere of paranoia created by terror attacks.[86] Indian Americans remind us that no matter how affluent and well educated an immigrant community might be, they can never take civil rights for granted; rather, they have to be constantly vigilant and protective of those rights. Although they are yet to gain political clout through the voting booth, Indian Americans are learning that there are other pathways in the American political process for representation that they must exploit more fully. These include presidential appointments

Diwali is a popular Hindu holiday celebrated by many Indian Americans. Known as the "Hindu Festival of Lights," the five-day celebration usually falls in late October or early November and ushers in the Hindu New Year. Pictured here is Denesh Kapoor, a high school student from Manassas Park, Virginia, who is lighting candles in honor of the celebration.

and commissions, coalitions with other groups who share the same interests and agenda, and strengthening of bonds between India and the United States.

THE WORLD IS ONE FAMILY

The concept of a global family is enshrined in the ancient Sanskrit phrase *Vasudeva Kutumbakam*, meaning "The World Is One Family." Looking at Indian Americans scattered across the world helps us understand them as a globalized community, an oikumene. They are an important part of a larger family of more than 25 million overseas Indians spread across 110 countries over five continents with an estimated combined income of $160 billion. This staggering amount is equal to 35 percent of

India's gross domestic product, making overseas Indians a critical part of the home country's economic development.[87]

This perspective on Indian Americans also reminds us that immigrants are connected not only to their immediate surroundings but also to far-flung countries. Whether it is Moola Singh grieving for the wife he had left behind in India, Congressman Dalip Singh Saund returning to his village in Punjab to spread the American message of equal opportunity, Chandra Lachman Singh going back to India to fight for independence from the British, or Gurmale Grewal taking annual trips to India with his family, the theme of human interconnectedness across oceans remains valid no matter what the historical period.

Indian immigrants have given new meaning to the terms *immigration* and *globalization*. By using the modern tools of technology to remain interconnected, they have shown us that we can no longer think in simplistic terms of immigrants as people who flee their homeland and settle down in the new country, never to look back. Such a history may have been true for immigrants who fled poverty and persecution in Europe or came as refugees from East Asia. For modern Indian immigrants, however, the reality is that they not only visit their homeland again and again, but they go back home to work and live, sometimes for long periods at a time. As such, they are true "transnationals," speaking many languages, comfortable in many cultures, across many continents. They use their wealth and education to make better lives for themselves and for others, both in the new country and in their homeland, to which they remain strongly connected.

There are many reasons why Indian Americans have been able to bring traditions from the homeland and transform them into a uniquely Indian-American culture. The freedom that India has given to its people to migrate, and the opportunities provided by U.S. immigration laws and American society, are both responsible for the Indian immigrant story. Selective as the 1965 immigration law was, allowing only the best-qualified and most highly skilled people to enter, it still permitted growth of the community through sponsoring of relatives. The experience of Indian Americans shows that allowing entire families to immigrate leads to stable family life and greater work productivity, and enables acculturation without loss of immigrant identity. Their well-being in America is dependent on continued good relations between India and the United States; the ability of Americans to abide by their liberal, pluralistic principles; and the desire of Indian Americans to grow and flourish as a distinct and valuable part of the American mosaic. When the terror strikes of September 11, 2001, led to greater immigration restrictions and more hostility toward immigrants from South Asia, it ruined the atmosphere and endangered the well-being, not only of immigrant groups but of American society itself.

The ups and downs of Indian-American history show us that, although there are always forces beyond our immediate control that affect our lives, we can do much to shape our own destinies. Individual and collective actions are both important in determining the course of our lives, and that, ultimately, is the best history lesson of all.

• Study Questions •

1. Has your overall understanding of Indian Americans changed after reading this book? If so, how?

2. What does the Indian-American experience teach us about
   (a) Adapting to a new culture?
   (b) Racism and discrimination?

3. How do you think Indian Americans would be affected if
   (a) Emigration from India suddenly dried up?
   (b) More and more immigrants kept coming from India?

(continues on next page)

(continued from previous page)

• Study Questions •

4. What factors might contribute to the increase or decrease of emigration from India?

5. If you were a member of the U.S. Congress, what kind of immigration laws would you pass?

Chronology

1820   The first and lone Indian is admitted to the United States and entered in immigration records.

1834   Britain abolishes slavery and recruits indentured Indian laborers to replace slaves in plantation colonies.

1900–1910   The first significant wave of immigrants from India to Canada and the United States brings more than 7,000 farmers, mostly Sikh, from Punjab to the Pacific Northwest.

1907   In the Bellingham (Washington) riots, civilian mobs turn violent and drive Indian workers out of town.

1910   In the *United States v. Balsara*, the Supreme Court rules that Indians are eligible for citizenship, because they are "Caucasian" like the "whites."

1913   California Alien Land Law prohibits aliens "ineligible to citizenship" from owning land or property but permits three-year leases; in 1920, the law is modified to prohibit leases.

1917   *September 18:* Immigration Act (or Barred Zone Act) establishes a "barred zone" to prevent immigrants from India and other East Asian countries from entering the United States.

1923   In a dramatic reversal, Supreme Court Justice George Sutherland rules in the *United States v. Bhagat Singh Thind* case that being "Caucasian" is not enough to be considered "white"; Indians are not "free white persons" and therefore are ineligible for citizenship.

133

1924   Immigration Act: a quota law that limits immigration to 2 percent of nationalities already in the United States, based on the 1890 U.S. census; the act prohibits immigration of aliens who are ineligible for citizenship, a category that includes Chinese, Japanese, Koreans, and Asian Indians.

1931   The Cable Act—which took away a white woman's citizenship if she married an alien ineligible for citizenship—is repealed.

1946   *May 24:* Luce-Cellar Bill grants citizenship rights to Asian Indians and Filipinos and establishes a quota of 100 immigrants per year from India and the Philippines.

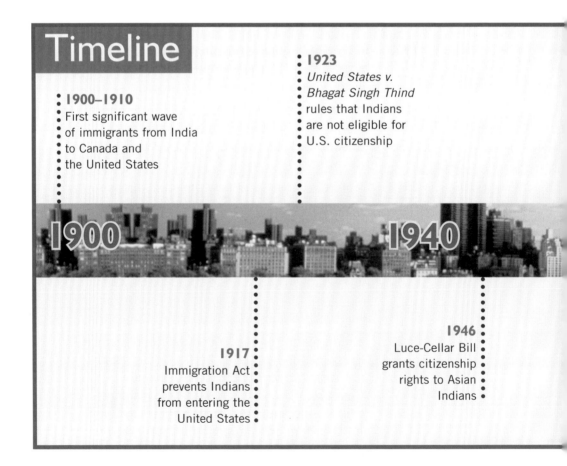

Timeline

1900–1910
First significant wave of immigrants from India to Canada and the United States

1923
United States v. Bhagat Singh Thind rules that Indians are not eligible for U.S. citizenship

1900   **1940**

1917
Immigration Act prevents Indians from entering the United States

1946
Luce-Cellar Bill grants citizenship rights to Asian Indians

1947   *August 15:* India wins independence after nearly 200 years of British rule.

1957   Dalip Singh Saund (D-California) becomes the first Asian and the first native of India to be elected to Congress.

1965   Immigration reforms reverse discriminatory quota law of 1924 and admit Asians in large numbers; the number of immigrants from any independent Asian country is raised to 20,000 with an annual limit of 170,000 from the Eastern hemisphere; preference is given to skilled professionals whose services are urgently needed in the United States and to immediate family members of U.S. citizens.

1957
Dalip Singh Saund becomes first native of India to be elected to Congress

1987
Navroze Mody is beaten to death by a gang of Hispanic and white youth in Hoboken, New Jersey

2004
Bobby Jindal elected to Congress

1960

2000

1965
Immigration and Naturalization Services Act reverses discriminatory quota law of 1924 and admits Asians in large numbers

2000
Indian-American population exceeds 1 million mark in the 2000 U.S. census

1980	Indians are counted in the U.S. census as "Asian Indians" for the first time in a separate group.
1986	Immigration and Reform Control Act enables certain undocumented aliens to become eligible for citizenship and makes it illegal to knowingly hire undocumented aliens.
1987	Indian American Navroze Mody is beaten to death by a gang of Hispanic and white youth in Hoboken, New Jersey, amidst a series of other violent hate crimes against Indian immigrants.
1990	United States begins to admit large numbers of Indians under H1B visas as skilled computer workers; information technology revolution leads to worldwide demand for skilled workers; India embarks on road to economic liberalization.
1997	Astronaut Kalpana Chawla becomes the first Indian American to embark on a space flight; she perishes along with her crewmembers on the space shuttle *Columbia* in February 2003.
2000	The Indian-American population crosses the 1 million mark in the 2000 U.S. census; the technology bubble bursts; outsourcing of white-collar work to India is hotly debated.
2001	The terror attacks of September 11 cast a cloud over immigrants from the Middle East and South Asia.
2004	Bobby Jindal becomes the first Indian-American Republican to be elected to Congress as a representative from Louisiana.

Notes

Chapter 1

1. Tarun Basu, "State Dinner for Prime Minister Manmohan Singh. 'Complete the Journey' of Columbus, PM tells U.S.," *DesiTALK*, July 22, 2005, 10.
2. Indrani Bagchi, "Indian Students in US Still No. 1," *The Times of India News Network*, November 10, 2004.
3. Statistics Canada, Visible Minority Population, Census of Population, 2001, Provinces and Territories.
4. N. C. SriRekha, "200,000 NRI Millionaires in U.S." *India Post*, May 23, 2003, 16.
5. "Indian Americans: They Matter," *India Today International*, October 2, 2000.
6. Joseph Berger, "For Indians in the U.S., Spelling Is Path to Top," *International Herald Tribune*, June 6, 2005.

Chapter 2

7. Lakshmi Menon, Padma Rangaswamy, Dorothie Shah, eds., *Asian Indians of Chicago*. Images of America Series (Chicago: Arcadia, 2003), 4.
8. Karen I. Leonard, *Making Ethnic Choices: California's Punjabi Mexican Americans* (Philadelphia: Temple University Press, 1992), 30.
9. Roger Daniels, *History of Indian Immigration to the United States. An Interpretive Essay* (New York: The Asia Society, 1989).
10. Ronald Takaki, *Strangers from a Different Shore: A History of Asian Americans* (Boston: Little, Brown, 1989), 309.
11. H. Brett Melendy, *Asians in America: Filipinos, Koreans, and East Indians* (Boston: Twayne, 1977), 231
12. Takaki, *Strangers from a Different Shore*, 307.
13. Leonard, *Making Ethnic Choices*, 150–157.
14. Ibid., 155.
15. Takaki, *Strangers from a Different Shore*, 299–300.
16. Melendy, *Asians in America*, 234.

Chapter 3

17. Available online at *www.worldfacts.us/india*.
18. Romilla Thapar, *Ancient Indian Social History* (New Delhi, India: Orient Longman Ltd.), 1978.
19. Percival Spear, *The Oxford History of Modern India, 1740–1975*

(Oxford: Oxford University Press), 1978.

20. Hugh Tinker, *A New System of Slavery: The Export of Indian Labour Overseas 1830–1920* (London: Oxford University Press), 1974.

21. Central Intelligence Agency Web site, available online at *www.cia.gov*.

22. Confederation of India Industry Web site, available online at *www.ciionline.org*.

23. CIA Website

Chapter 4

24. Padma Rangaswamy, *The Imperatives of Choice and Change: Post-1965 Immigrants from India in Metropolitan Chicago* (Ph.D. Dissertation, University of Illinois at Chicago, 1996), 520.

25. Padma Rangaswamy, *Namasté America: Indian Immigrants in an American Metropolis* (University Park, Pa.: Pennsylvania State University Press, 2000), 150.

26. Menon, et al., *Asian Indians of Chicago*, 17.

27. Rangaswamy, *Namasté America*, 148.

28. Ibid., 149.

29. David Reimers, *Still the Golden Door: The Third World Comes to America* (New York: Columbia University Press, 1992), 95.

30. Rangaswamy, *Namasté America*, 149.

31. Ibid., 199.

32. Rangaswamy, *The Imperatives of Choice and Change*, 471.

33. Ibid., 458.

34. Rangaswamy, *Namasté America*, 236.

35. Rangaswamy, *Namasté America*, 279.

36. Table 25. Nonimmigrants Admitted as Temporary Workers, Exchange Visitors, and Intracompany Transferees by Region and Country of Citizenship: Fiscal Year 2004, available online at *www.uscis.gov*.

Chapter 5

37. "A Demographic Overview, 1996 Census," available online at *www.pch.gc.ca/multicultural-canada*

38. Lavina Melwani, "Indian Majority," in *Little India* (New York: Little India Publications, October 2005), 34.

39. Chidanand Rajghatta, "The Billionaires," in *The Indian Express, North American Edition* (September 29, 2000).

40. Rangaswamy, *Namasté America*, 154.

41. Rangaswamy, *Namasté America*, 175.

42. Ibid., 208–209.

43. Anita Gupta, "Voices of a New Generation," in *Little India* (New York: Little India Publications. March 2004), 18–20.

Chapter 6

44. Prema Kurien, "Becoming American by Becoming Hindu:

Indian Americans Take Their Place at the Multicultural Table" in *Gatherings in Diaspora: Religious Communities and the New Generation*, eds. R. Stephen Warner and Judith G. Wittner (Philadelphia: Temple University Press, 1998), 53.

45. Available online at *www.aapiusa.org*

46. Available online at *www.aahoa.org*

47. "NRIs Create Jobs in Silicon Valley," *Economic Times*, May 27, 2004.

48. Available online at *www.tie.org*

49. Available online at *www.midwestcricket.org*

50. "South Asian World, Channel for S. Asians, Available on DISH Network Platform," *News India-Times*, December 24, 2004, 23.

Chapter 7

51. Rangaswamy, *Namasté America*, 174.

52. Ibid., 175.

53. Ramiza Shamoun Koya, "Chicken Curry, or a Brief History of My Life as an Indian," in *Catamaran: South Asian American Writing* (Storrs, Conn.: University of Connecticut, Asian American Studies Institute) Vol. 2 (Fall 2004).

54. Sunaina Marr Maira, *Desis in the House: Indian American Youth Culture in New York City* (Philadephia: Temple University Press, 2002).

55. Ibid., 153.

56. S. Thaker, "Manager/Wife: Indian Women in the Motel Business," *Committee on South Asian Women Bulletin 5*, no.1 (1987): 19–20

57. Rangaswamy, *The Imperatives of Choice and Change*, 474–475.

58. Madhulika Kandelwal, *Becoming American, Being Indian: An Immigrant Community in New York City. (*Ithaca, N.Y.: Cornell University Press, 2002), 172.

59. South Asian American Leaders of Tomorrow (SAALT), *American Backlash: Terrorists Bring War Home in More Ways than One*, 2001.

60. Rangaswamy, *Namasté America*, 179.

Chapter 8

61. Rangaswamy, *Namasté America*, 294.

62. "Indian Americans Much Sought-after Group in U.S. Polls" October 25, 2004, available online at *www.economictimes.com*.

63. Ibid.

64. Multiculturalism: A Canada for All: Canada's Action Plan against Racism—An Overview, available online at *www.pch.gc.ca*.

65. Available online at *www.indocanadian.com*.

66. Nancy Liu, "A Political Wake-up Call for Indian Americans: Outsourcing Debate Casts New Light on New Homeland," April

19, 2004, available online at *www.msnbc.com*.

67. Available online at *www.indo-american.org*.

68. Manavi (New Jersey), Sakhi (New York), Apna Ghar (Chicago), and Maitri (San Francisco) are some of the shelters for South Asian women in the major cities.

69. M.K.G. Pillai (1924–1974) cofounded the Indo-American Center and was elected to Chicago's Hall of Fame for Senior Citizens in 1992, available online at *www.indoamerican.org*.

70. *Little India*, July 2005, available online at *www.littleindia.com*.

71. Available online at *www.sawnet.org*.

72. *News India-Times*, October 15, 2005, 31.

73. Available online at *www.leadershipforchange.org*.

Chapter 9

74. Available online at *www.sawnet.org*.

75. Available online at *www.nobelprize.org*.

76. Available online at *www.imagine.gsfc.nasa.gov*.

77. Available online at *www.english.emory.edu/Bahri/Ramanujan.html*.

78. Available online at *www.saaja.org*.

79. Available online at *www.english.emory.edu/Bahri/Mukherjee.html*.

80. Available online at *www.pch.gc.ca* (Canadians of Asian heritage who inspire us).

81. Available online at *www.pga.com*.

82. Available online at *www.asian-athletes.com*.

Chapter 10

83. Available online at *www.singhweb.com*

84. Barbara Kantrowitz and Julie Scelfo, "American Masala," *Newsweek*, March 22, 2005.

85. Indian American Friendship Council's posting of Bill Clinton's letter to Indian Americans on Diwali 2000. President Clinton, who enjoys Indian food, was the first president to have an official Diwali celebration in the White House, with chefs dishing up his favorite Indian menu. Available online at *www.iafc.us*.

86. Anil Padmanabhan, "Unequal Terms," *India Today International*, November 23, 2003.

87. "Of Brain Gain and Homecoming" *Times of India* (online), January 10, 2005.

Glossary

Ayurveda   Ancient system of Indian medicine.

Bala Vihar   Hindu youth group formed for spiritual study.

Bhangra   Vigorous Punjabi folk dance.

Bharatanatyam   Classical South Indian dance.

bindi   Decorative dot worn by South Asian women on their forehead.

Brahman   Supreme Hindu godhead.

Brahmin   Highest caste category of priests.

dandia-ras/garba   Popular Gujarati folk dance with sticks.

Desi   Belonging to one's country (used by South Asians).

dharma   Duty or obligation.

Diwali   Hindu festival of Lights.

Ghadr   "Revolutionary" party of Indian freedom, formed in California.

gurdwara   Sikh house of worship.

henna/mehendi   Vegetable dye used for "temporary tattoo" decorations.

karma   Actions to carry out one's duty.

Kathak   North Indian classical dance.

Kshatriya   Warrior caste or the caste of kings.

kurta   Loose shirt worn by Indian men.

Mahabharata   Grand Hindu philosophical epic with story of Krishna.

masala   A unique blend of spices used in Indian cooking.

moksha   Release from the cycle of birth and rebirth.

Navratri   Hindu festival of nine nights celebrated with music and dance.

nirvana   Culmination of existence or release of the soul into nonexistence.

oikumene   A global household, including a homeland and those who live outside it.

Ramayana   Hindu epic centered upon the King Rama.

salwar kameez   Shirt and trouser outfit worn by Punjabi women.

sari   Traditional Indian women's clothing, 6 to 9 yards (5 1/2 to 8 1/4 meters) long.

Sudra   Lowest caste of menial workers.

Untouchable   At the bottom of society and outside the caste hierarchy.

Vaisya   The merchant caste.

Vedas   The oldest Sanskrit texts of Hinduism.

Bibliography

Bacon, Jean. *Life Lines: Community, Family, and Assimilation Among Asian Indian Immigrants*. Oxford: Oxford University Press, 1996.

Brass, Paul R. "The Politics of India Since Independence," in Gordon Johnson, ed. *The New Cambridge History of India,* vol. 4.1. Cambridge, UK: Cambridge University Press, 1989.

Brown, Richard Harvey, and George V. Coelho, eds. *Tradition and Transformation: Asian Indians in America*. Studies in Third World Societies 38. Williamsburg, Va.: College of William and Mary, 1986.

Buchignani, Norman, and Doreen M. Indra, with Ram Srivastava. *Continuous Journey: A Social History of South Asians in Canada*. Toronto: McClelland and Stewart Ltd., 1985.

Chandrasekhar, S. ed. *From India to America: A Brief History of Immigration: Problems of Discrimination, Admission & Assimilation*. La Jolla, Calif.: Population Review, 1982.

Clarke, Colin, Ceri Peach, and Steven Vertovec, eds. *South Asians Overseas: Migration and Ethnicity*. Cambridge, UK: Cambridge University Press, 1990.

Daniels, Roger. *History of Indian Immigration to the United States: An Interpretive Essay*. New York: The Asia Society, 1989.

Fenton, John Y. *Transplanting Religious Traditions: Asian Indians in America*. New York: Praeger, 1988.

Fisher, Maxine P. *The Indians of New York City: A Study of Immigrants from India*. Columbia, Mo.: South Asia Books, 1980.

Helweg, Arthur W., and Usha M. Helweg. *An Immigrant Success Story: East Indians in America*. Philadelphia: University of Pennsylvania Press, 1991.

Jain, Ravindra K. *Indian Communities Abroad: Themes and Literature*. New Delhi, India: Manohar Publishers, 1993.

Jensen, Joan M. *Passage from India: Asian Indian Immigrants in North America.* New Haven, Conn.: Yale University Press, 1988.

Khandelwal, Madhulika S. *Becoming American, Being Indian: An Immigrant Community in New York City.* Ithaca, N.Y.: Cornell University Press, 2002.

Kitano, Harry H. L., and Roger Daniels. *Asian Americans: Emerging Minorities.* Upper Saddle River, N.J.: Prentice Hall, 1988.

Koya, Ramiza Shamoun. "Chicken Curry, or a Brief History of My Life as an Indian" *Catamaran: South Asian American Writing* (University of Connecticut, Asian American Studies Institute) vol. 2 (Fall 2004).

Kurien, Prema. "Becoming American by Becoming Hindu: Indian Americans Take Their Place at the Multicultural Table," in R. Stephen Warner and Judith G. Wittner, eds. *Gatherings in Diaspora: Religious Communities and the New Generation.* Philadelphia: Temple University Press, 1998.

Leonard, Karen I. *Making Ethnic Choices: California's Punjabi Mexican Americans.* Philadelphia: Temple University Press, 1992.

———. *The South Asian Americans.* The New Americans Series. Westport, Conn.: Greenwood Press, 1997.

Maira, Sunaina Marr. *Desis in the House: Indian American Youth Culture in New York City.* Philadelphia: Temple University Press, 2002.

Majumdar, R.C., and P. N. Chopra. *Main Currents of Indian History,* 2nd ed. New Delhi, India: Sterling, 1994.

Melendy, H. Brett. *Asians in America: Filipinos, Koreans, and East Indians.* Boston: Twayne, 1977.

Motwani, Jagat K., Mahin Gosine, and Jyoti Barot, eds. *Global Indian Diaspora: Yesterday, Today and Tomorrow.* New York: Global Organization of People of Indian Origin, 1993.

Nehru, Jawaharlal. *The Discovery of India.* New Delhi, India: Oxford University Press, 1982. First published in Calcutta: The Signet Press, 1946.

Prashad, Vijay. "Crafting Solidarities," in Lavina Dhingra Shankar and Rajini Srikanth, eds. *A Part, Yet Apart.* Philadelphia: Temple University Press, 1998.

Rangaswamy, Padma. "Asian Indians in Chicago: Growth and Change in a Model Minority," in Melvin J. Holli and Peter d'A. Jones, eds. *Ethnic Chicago: A Multicultural Portrait*. Grand Rapids, Mich.: William B. Eerdmans, 1995, pp. 438–462.

——. "Dalip Singh Saund," in *Asian American Encyclopedia*. Pasadena, Calif.: Salem Press, 1995.

——. *The Imperatives of Choice and Change: Post-1965 Immigrants from India in Metropolitan Chicago*. Ph.D. Dissertation, University of Illinois at Chicago, 1996.

——. *Namasté America: Indian Immigrants in an American Metropolis*. University Park, Pa.: Pennsylvania State University Press, 2000.

——, and Dorothie Shah. *Asian Immigration to the United States: A Unit of Study for Grades 8–12*. Los Angeles: University of California, The National Center for History in the Schools, 2001.

Reimers, David M. *Still the Golden Door: The Third World Comes to America*. New York: Columbia University Press, 1992.

Saran, Paramatma. *The Asian Indian Experience in the United States*. Cambridge, Mass.: Schenkman, 1985.

Schelbert, Leo. "Emigration from Imperial Germany Overseas, 1871–1914: Contours, Contexts, Experiences," in Volker Duis, Kathy Harms, and Peter Hayes, eds. *Imperial Germany*, pp. 109–133. Madison, Wisc.: University of Wisconsin Press, 1985.

Shah, Sonia. "Three Hot Meals and a Full Day at Work" in Shamita Das Gupta, ed., *A Patchwork Shawl: Chronicles of South Asian Women in America*. New Brunswick, N.J.: Rutgers University Press, 1998, pp. 206–221.

Spear, Percival. *The Oxford History of Modern India, 1740–1975*. Oxford: Oxford University Press, 1978.

Statistics Canada, Visible Minority Population, Census of Population, 2001, Provinces and Territories.

Takaki, Ronald. *Strangers from a Different Shore: A History of Asian Americans*. Boston: Little, Brown, 1989.

Thapar, Romila. *Ancient Indian Social History*. New Delhi, India: Orient Longman Ltd., 1978.

Tinker, Hugh. *A New System of Slavery: The Export of Indian Labour Overseas 1830–1920*. London: Oxford University Press, 1974.

———. *The Banyan Tree: Overseas Emigrants from India, Pakistan and Bangladesh*. London: Oxford University Press, 1977.

Williams, Raymond B. *Religions of Immigrants from India and Pakistan: New Threads in the American Tapestry*. Cambridge, UK: Cambridge University Press, 1988.

———, ed. *A Sacred Thread: Modern Transmission of Hindu Traditions in India and Abroad*. Chambersburg, Pa.: Anima Publications, 1992.

Wolpert, Stanley. *An Introduction to India*. Berkeley, Calif.: University of California Press, 1991; New Delhi: Penguin Books, 1994.

NEWSPAPERS AND MAGAZINES

Bagchi, Indrani. "Indian Students in US Still No. 1," *The Times of India News Network*. November 10, 2004.

Basu, Tarun. "State Dinner for Prime Minister Manmohan Singh. 'Complete the Journey' of Columbus, PM Tells U.S.," *DesiTALK*, July 22, 2005.

Berger, Joseph. "For Indians in the U.S., Spelling Is Path to Top," *International Herald Tribune*. June 6, 2005.

Gupta, Anita. "Voices of a New Generation," in *Little India* (March 2004). Available online at *http://www.littleindia.com/february 2003/Voices%20of%20a%20New%20Generation.htm*.

"Indian Americans Much Sought-after Group in U.S. Polls." October 25, 2004. Available online at *www.economictimes.com*.

"Indian Americans: They Matter." *India Today International*, October 2, 2000.

Kantrowitz, Barbara, and Julie Scelfo, "American Masala," *Newsweek*, March 22, 2005.

Lak, Daniel. South Asian News, *BBC Despatches from Delhi*. November 20, 1997.

Liu, Nancy. "A Political Wake-up Call for Indian Americans: Outsourcing Debate Casts New Light on New Homeland." MSNBC, April 19, 2004. Available online at *www.msnbc.com*.

Melwani, Lavina. "Indian Majority," in *Little India*, October 2005. Available online at *www.littleindia.com/october2005/IndianMajority.htm*.

"NRIs Create Jobs in Silicon Valley." *Economic Times*. May 27, 2004.

"Of Brain Gain and Homecoming." *Times of India* (online), January 10, 2005.

Padmanabhan, Anil. "Unequal Terms." *India Today International*, November 23, 2003.

Rajghatta, Chidanand. "The Billionaires." *The Indian Express North American Edition*, September 29, 2000.

"South Asian World, Channel for S. Asians, Available on DISH Network Platform." *News India-Times*, December 24, 2004, 23.

SriRekha, N. C. "200,000 NRI Millionaires in U.S." *India Post*, May 23, 2003, 16.

WEB SITES

Asian American Hotel Owners Association
www.aahoa.com.

American Physicians of Indian Origin
www.aapiusa.org/index.aspx.

Asian Athletes
www.asianathletes.com.

Central Intelligence Agency
www.cia.gov.

Confederation of Indian Industry
www.ciionline.org.

Emory University Department of English
www.english.emory.edu.

Indian American Friendship Council
www.iafc.us.

Indo-American Center
www.indoamerican.org.

Indo-Canadian Community
www.indocanadian.com.

Leadership for a Changing World
www.leadershipforchange.org.

Little India Magazine
www.littleindia.com.

Midwest Cricket Association
www.midwestcricket.org.

National Aeronautics Space Agency
www.nasa.gov.

The Nobel Prize
www.nobelprize.org.

Government of Canada
www.pch.gc.ca/multiculturalcanada.

Professional Golfers' Association
www.pga.com.

South Asian American Journalists Association
www.saaja.org.

South Asian Women's Network
www.sawnet.org.

The Indus Entrepreneurs
www.tie.org.

U.S. Census
www.uscis.gov.

Further Reading

Daswani, Kavita. *The Village Bride of Beverly Hills*. New York: Putnam, 2004.

Hidier, Tanuja Desai. *Born Confused*. New York: PUSH, an imprint of Scholastic, Inc., 2002.

Indo-American Center, *Asian Indians of Chicago*. Images of America Series. Lakshmi Menon, Padma Rangaswamy, Dorothie Shah, eds. Chicago: Arcadia Publishing, 2003.

Kalita, S. Mitra. *Suburban Sahibs: Three Immigrant Families and Their Passage from India to America*. New Brunswick, N.J.: Rutgers University Press, 2003.

Kamdar, Mira. *Motiba's Tattoos: A Granddaughter's Journey into Her Indian Family's Past*. New York: Public Affairs, 2000.

Lessinger, Johanna. *From the Ganges to the Hudson: Indian Immigrants in New York City*. New Immigrants Series. Needham Heights, Mass.: Allyn and Bacon, 1995.

McDaniel, Jan. *Indian Immigration: Changing Face of North America*. Broomall, Pa.: Mason Crest Publishers, 2004.

WEB SITES

There are literally hundreds of Web sites serving the Indian-American community. They cover a wide range of interests, from matchmaking (*www.bharatmatrimony.com*) to religion (*www.hindutemples.us*) to violence against women (*www.hindustan.net*). A Google search on any specific subject with the addition of the words "South Asian" or "Asian Indian" will bring up relevant Web sites. Unfortunately, the term Indian American tends to bring up American Indian or Native American references, so it is best to use terms like *Indian immigrants* or *Indian diaspora* when doing a search. Listed below are some newspaper/magazine/informational Web sites popular with Indian Americans:

Links to major Indian-American Newspapers and Magazines
http://www.allied-media.com/Publications/indian_newspapers_
US.htm

Newsmagazine for South Asians in Canada
www.canadiandesi.ca

Chicago's Northside Asian Indian Community
http://www.chicagohistory.org/global/iasian.html

Pennsylvania's New Immigrants
http://www.hsp.org/default.aspx?id=107

University of California, Berkeley's South Asia Resource Center
www.lib.berkeley.edu/SSEAL/SouthAsia

Number One Portal for South Asians in the United States
www.planetguru.com

India Abroad
www.rediff.com

Connecting Indians Worldwide
www.sulekha.com

Picture Credits

Index

About the Contributors

Series Editor **Robert D. Johnston** is associate professor and director of the Teaching of History Program in the Department of History at the University of Illinois at Chicago. He is the author of *The Making of America: The History of the United States from 1492 to the Present*, a middle-school textbook that received a School Library Journal Best Book of the Year award. He is currently working on a history of vaccine controversies in American history, to be published by Oxford University Press.

Padma Rangaswamy is cofounder and director of the South Asian American Policy and Research Institute (SAAPRI) in Chicago, Illinois. She is the author of *Namasté America: Indian Immigrants in an American Metropolis* and has contributed several entries to encyclopedias on world immigrant cultures, Asian American history, and world diaspora history. Rangaswamy is an active member of Chicago's Indian-American community and has taught World History, American History, and Asian-American History at many universities.